THE CHILEAN SENATE

INTERNAL DISTRIBUTION OF INFLUENCE

T0324397

Latin American Monographs, No. 23
Institute of Latin American Studies
The University of Texas at Austin

THE CHILEAN SENATE

Internal Distribution of Influence

by Weston H. Agor

PUBLISHED FOR THE *Institute of Latin American Studies*
BY THE UNIVERSITY OF TEXAS PRESS • AUSTIN

ISBN 978-0-292-76835-2
Library of Congress Catalog Card Number 79-165918
© 1971 By Weston H. Agor
Type set by G&S Typesetters, Austin

.   .

utpress.utexas.edu/index.php/rp-form

For EUGENE GARRETT BEWKES

who inspired me to continue and ultimately

complete my graduate education

PREFACE

METHODOLOGICALLY, this study of the Chilean Senate employs theoretical approaches originally developed by Richard F. Fenno, Jr., John F. Manley, and John Wahlke and his associates to understand and explain the U.S. House Appropriations Committee, the House Ways and Means Committee, and four state legislatures, respectively.[1] Accordingly, several of their questions were translated word for word and incorporated in an overall interview schedule including questions originally written by the author to quantify phenomena unique to the Chilean Senate and perhaps to a few other Latin American legislatures (see Appendix B).

Some readers may believe that this methodological approach is inappropriate for the study of Latin American legislatures and reflects an ethnocentric bias that defines a "developed" political system as one that resembles the existing institutional structure of North America or Western Europe.[2] They would also probably argue with Samuel Huntington that such institutions have no meaning in Latin America, and that "the variations of the North American political system which North Americans would like to reproduce in Latin America are simply too weak, too diffuse, too dispersed to mobilize the political power neces-

[1] Richard F. Fenno, Jr., *The Power of the Purse: Appropriations Politics in Congress*; John F. Manley, "The House Committee on Ways and Means: 1947–1966" (Ph.D. dissertation, Syracuse University, 1967); John Wahlke *et al.*, *The Legislative System: Explorations in Legislative Behavior*.

[2] See, for example, Charles W. Anderson, Fred R. von der Mehden, and Crawford Young, *Issues of Political Development*, p. 7.

sary to bring about fundamental change."[3] Although Huntington's conclusions appear appropriate for most of Latin America, readers are reminded that Chile stands out as a deviant case. Politically, Chile compares favorably with many of the developed political systems of Western Europe[4] and, on one recent index, ranked ahead of the United
States.[5]

As far as Latin American legislatures are concerned, Huntington
may be correct to conclude that they "are dominated by landlords" and
that a "basic incompatibility exists between parliaments and land reform." It is significant to note, however, that the Chilean Congress is
one of the few legislative systems in the developing world that passed
a land reform law in the 1960's, as well as other important legislation.
Furthermore, although it may be true that "legislatures are more conservative than executives,"[6] a balanced appraisal of Chile's recent history does not produce such clear-cut conclusions.

It is my contention that, although the methodological approaches
used to analyze and understand the North American polity may be
irrelevant to most of Latin America, they are relevant to Chile. Just as
the U.S. model is a rarity as a political system on the world scene, so is
the Chilean political system, which is patterned after it. Similarly, although a Tudor polity may be incompatible with most of Latin America, it may well be compatible with the Chilean society at its relatively
advanced stage of political and cultural development and its transitional
stage of economic development.

Accordingly, methodological approaches used to analyze and understand the U.S. Congress may be irrelevant in a study of most Latin
American legislatures, but they appear to be productive techniques in

[3] Samuel P. Huntington, *Political Order in Changing Societies*, p. 136.

[4] William Flanigan and Edwin Fogleman, "Patterns of Political Development and
Democratization: A Quantitative Analysis" (Paper delivered at the 1967 Annual
Meeting of the American Political Science Association, Chicago, September 5–9,
1967), fig. 6 between pp. 13 and 14.

[5] Robert A. Dahl, "The Evaluation of Political Systems," in *Contemporary Political Science: Toward Empirical Theory*, ed. Ithiel de Sola Pool, p. 173.

[6] Huntington, *Political Order in Changing Societies*, pp. 358, 388.

the study of the Chilean Senate. It would be inappropriate to apply these techniques in a study of most Latin American legislatures; it would be just as inappropriate *not* to apply them in a study of the Chilean Senate.

I would like to acknowledge the assistance of several people who contributed substantially to this book. Professors John F. Manley, Charles W. Anderson, and John Strasma not only made important suggestions before I entered the field, but subsequently read the entire manuscript and suggested improvements. Dr. Manley's advice on other personal matters is also greatly appreciated. Allan Kornberg and Lloyd Musolf made comments on the introductory chapter of this book, and Federico G. Gil's and Charles Parrish's correspondence stimulated me to make further improvements.

The author would also like to thank the senators and staff members (particularly Pedro Correa Opaso, Jorge Tapia Valdés, Iván Auger Labarca, Rodemil Torres Vásquez, Rafael Eyzaguirre Echeverría, Luis Valencia Avaria, Raúl Charlin Vicuña, and members of the Office of Information of the Senate) who gave so freely of their time. Members of the statistics and archives departments of the Superintendencia de Compañías de Seguros, Sociedades Anónimas y Bolsas de Comercio y Bancos provided useful data.

The Edward John Noble Foundation provided fellowship support for Spanish training prior to my trip to Chile on a Fulbright grant in 1962–1963. A National Defense Education Act Title VI fellowship enabled me to continue language and area studies at the University of Wisconsin in 1966–1967, and the Midwest Universities Consortium and the Land Tenure Center of the University of Wisconsin provided thesis support on different occasions.

My Chilean wife, Eliana Bauer de Agor, deserves special thanks. Her observations, particularly in the field, were invaluable. Also, I am grateful to Mrs. Lloyd Renneberg, who typed the entire manuscript and made several helpful suggestions for improvement, and to Warren Dean, former chairman of the Publications Committee of the Institute of Latin American Studies, The University of Texas at Austin, who guided the final publication process to completion. Translations from interviews and Spanish texts and documents are mine. The responsibility for errors of fact or interpretation in this study is mine alone.

Portions of this work originally appeared in Allan Kornberg and Lloyd Musolf (eds.), *Legislatures in Developmental Perspective* (Durham: Duke University Press, 1970), M. Donald Hancock and Herbert Hirsch (eds.), *Comparative Legislative Systems* (Glencoe, Ill.: The Free Press, 1971), and *The Journal of Latin American Studies* 2 (May, 1970) and are used here with their permission.

CONTENTS

INTRODUCTION

CONTEXT OF THE STUDY

A familiar theme in contemporary writings on comparative politics is the decline of legislatures or their lack of influence in the political system in the first place. For example, Carl J. Friedrich notes that, although parliaments held the center of the stage until World War I, the executive is now becoming the core of modern government. Leon N. Lindberg suggests that in most European countries, parliaments "neither make laws nor exercise effective control over the executive," and Robert Packenham concludes, "There is little evidence that more than a mere handful of national legislatures in the world have decision-making as their principal functions."[1] Many have even argued that the U.S. Congress's influence has declined in recent years.[2]

Certainly a good deal more legislative research is needed before such sweeping generalizations can be made. For example, political science research (traditional as well as empirical) on Latin American legislatures is glaringly inadequate. Robert E. Scott's survey of the literature

---

[1] Carl J. Friedrich, *Constitutional Government and Democracy*, rev. ed., p. 296; Leon N. Lindberg, "The Role of the European Parliament in an Emerging European Community," in *Lawmakers in a Changing World*, ed. Elke Frank, p. 110. (see also his footnote 13 for other excellent sources on European parliaments); Robert A. Packenham, "Legislatures and Political Development," in *Legislatures in Developmental Perspective*, ed. Allan Kornberg and Lloyd Musolf, p. 546.

[2] Samuel P. Huntington, "Congressional Responses to the Twentieth Century," in *The Congress and America's Future*, ed. David B. Truman.

in 1958 led him to conclude, "There is no general discussion of the Latin American congress in English, except for short statements in selected textbooks."[3] This is largely the result of the equally deficient country-by-country study of legislatures on which comparative analysis and theory must eventually be constructed.[4] As far as Chile is concerned, treatment is sparse and frequently legalistic. Federico Gil's most recent contribution in English, *The Political System of Chile*, contains only a brief discussion of Congress that relies on dated sources.

SCOPE OF THE STUDY

This study attempts to help fill this gap in the literature. It examines only the upper house of the Chilean Congress—the Senate—and even then represents only the first of the many studies required to describe and understand this chamber.

The primary focus is inside the Senate, where we seek to describe and analyze the internal distribution of influence: (1) the formal decision-making structure (committees and party structure), and (2) internal processes, both formal and informal, that hold the decision-making structure together. This approach is used because it helps to explain why and how the Senate exercises real influence in the decision-making process in Chile and how it contributes to the Chilean political system's persistence and stability.

More specifically, the Senate may be visualized as a political system imbedded in an environment, the most salient feature of which is a multiparty system. Because no single party normally commands a majority of the votes necessary for decision-making, the Senate serves as one arena where political parties meet, compromise, and agree on majority decisions on major legislation. But this process is complicated by the fact that, although there is an enormous area of agreement among Chilean political parties on certain policy objectives,[5] there is sharp

---

[3] Robert E. Scott, "Legislatures and Legislation," in *Government and Politics in Latin America*, ed. Harold Eugene Davis, p. 332.

[4] This gap in the literature also accounts in part for Latin America's frequent isolation from the mainstream of comparative politics, aptly noted by Merle Kling, "The State of Research in Latin America: Political Science," in *Social Science Research on Latin America*, ed. Charles Wagley, pp. 168–213.

[5] K. H. Silvert, "The Prospects of Chilean Democracy: Some Propositions on

disagreement on many others, including the means of implementation. The Senate as an institutional system is faced with the organizational problem of establishing an internal structure of influence able to form majority decisions across ideologically opposed political parties without tearing itself apart. This centers our attention on the structural elements of the Senate that enable it to cope with its environment by regulating its own internal behavior[6] and on the functional relationship between these mechanisms and the stability of Chile's political system.

One may justifiably ask at this point, "How do you know that the Senate exercises influence in the total political system and is therefore worthy of intensive study?" Robert Packenham rightly criticizes Wahlke, Eulau, Buchanan, and Ferguson's comparative study of state legislatures, *The Legislative System*, for assuming that legislatures have functions comprehensible above all as "lawmaking." He contends that the scholar should determine first, by empirical inquiry, that a legislature has influence in the political system before he spends time studying the internal structure and mechanisms of a legislature.[7]

In the context of world legislative experience, the Chilean Senate does exercise real influence in decision-making. There are factors that help to explain this: (1) the long evolutionary historical development of the Senate over 150 years; (2) the presence of an opposition majority in one of the two chambers, usually the Senate; (3) public support for a democratic system that includes a congress independent of the executive; (4) member stability and informal norms of Chamber-Senate apprenticeship and hard work in standing committees comparable to that in the U.S. Senate; and (5) senators' personal ties (economic and kinship) to the environment of the Senate system.

The internal distribution of influence of the Senate derives primarily from standing committees and their relationship to national political party leadership. Committees enjoy an autonomous base of influence

---

Chile," in *Latin American Politics: 24 Studies on the Contemporary Scene*, ed. Robert D. Tomasek, p. 396.

[6] This conceptual approach was first used by Richard F. Fenno, Jr., to describe the internal distribution of influence of the U.S. House of Representatives and is adapted here to fit the Chilean Senate. See Richard F. Fenno, Jr., "The Internal Distribution of Influence: The House," in *The Congress and America's Future*, ed. Truman.

[7] Packenham, "Legislature and Political Development," p. 110.

in relation to the leadership of national political parties, although the level of autonomy is somewhat below that for U.S. congressional committees. More specifically, political party discipline is limited to certain specific issues, and even then considerable slippage occurs. Also, Senate committees act as a center for decision-making on some key and most middle- and lower-range issues of importance by providing an environment in which norms of expertise, specialization, reciprocity, deference, and consideration of the national interest temper norms of partisanship—thereby permitting interparty compromise and agreement.

The ranking of committees—that is, which committees are more important, which less important, and why; the change in order over time; and conditions under which the ordering varies—is based, in this study, on senator and staff interview statements. Additional indicators that support these statements include, among others, the number of reports issued by each committee and the number of years of congressional experience members of top committees have compared with members of other committees. How committee seats and presidencies are assigned among political parties, how senators are recruited by party for each committee, how intraparty fights over key seats are resolved, and how often and why membership of committees change *within* each legislative period (four years) also reveal how influence is distributed inside the Senate. The role of the presidency of standing committees, its relation to committee staff, and the normative expectations that define boundaries of accepted behavior are further indicators.

The structure of political party leadership and its relationship to the presiding officer of the Senate pose special problems. Each government party that seeks to pass its program through the Senate is faced with the problem of building a majority in the multiparty environment; this is further complicated by a committee system with an intermediate level of autonomy apart from national party leadership. Four mechanisms composing the legislative leadership structure that help to provide the interparty cooperation and compromise necessary for majority decision-making are: the nonpartisan role of the president of the Senate, interparty conferences to work out floor procedures and policy agreements, floor leaders, and party caucuses. A final method of majority-building is the government party's (PDC) triparty arrangement to enhance policy coordination and development among congressional caucuses, the national party leadership, and the executive branch.

Throughout our review of the committee and party leadership structure of the Chilean Senate, several norms that define member and leadership roles and set minimum standards of expected behavior are analyzed. Frequently, these norms weaken partisanship and encourage interparty compromise. These formal and informal Senate norms of behavior facilitate the formation of interparty majorities and hold the decision-making structure together. More specifically, the Senate is guided by a body of formal rules, past precedents, and the Constitution. The Senate Rules, which govern most day to day procedures, are divided into four groups: committees, sessions and calendars, control of debate, and voting. But an analysis of informal rules is also necessary to understand fully Senate behavior. We find a system of informal norms that are widely held and observed across parties and that compare closely with those of the U.S. Senate. The relationship between the Senate's internal structure of influence and the longevity and balance of Chile's political system is largely the result of the successful operation of all these elements within the Senate.

Method and Data of the Study

Richard F. Fenno, Jr., defines the role of theory: "To guide the collection, interpretation, and presentation of facts . . . to help chart the terrain inside the Congress, to point up relevant kinds of relationships and to suggest directions for further research."[8] Prior to leaving for Chile, and with Fenno's definition in mind, we consciously set out to familiarize ourselves with as many theoretical approaches and legislative studies employing them as possible. The objective was to provide maximum conceptual flexibility and adaptability in the field. That is, familiarity with a large body of literature (it was hoped) would enable us to decide intelligently whether, when, and where a particular approach or approaches would be useful in guiding our study of the

[8] Richard F. Fenno, Jr., *The Power of the Purse: Appropriations Politics in Congress*, p. 680.

Senate, and perhaps would even aid us in developing our own scheme, if necessary.

Based on some previous knowledge of the Chilean political system acquired as a Fulbright Scholar in 1962–1963, I was optimistic about the possibility of employing such theoretical approaches as role, power, and exchange theory so effectively used by scholars to understand and explain legislative behavior in the United States.[9] But I had no real commitment to any particular body of theory and certainly was prepared to pick and choose or to reject all or any theoretical concepts and frameworks.

This study is based on the assumption that an eclectic use of both theory and method will be useful in isolating and describing important relationships in legislative processes, as well as in pointing out similarities and differences cross-nationally.[10] For example, role theory is used to analyze and describe how the president of the Senate and presidents of standing committees are expected to act in order to win the respect and support of their colleagues, and exchange theory in order to pinpoint why many senators seek to serve on important committees. Interviews are used to help map the internal distribution of influence, and analysis of debates, Office of Information (OIS) studies, and other documents are used to cross-check the accuracy of interview comments and perceptions. Role theory is also used to show the remarkable resemblance of Chilean and U.S. Senate norms in both content and function. On the other hand, theories of power and role are *also* employed to isolate the differences between institutional roles and expectations, as, for example, when comparing the presidency of a Chilean Senate committee with that of a chairmanship of U.S. congressional committees.

The principal data sources on which this study is based are: interviews in the field (forty-three of the total forty-five senators [1968],

9 For example, see Donald R. Matthews, *U.S. Senators and Their World*, ch. 5; John F. Manley, "The House Committee on Ways and Means: 1947–1966" (Ph.D. dissertation, Syracuse University, 1967), pp. 5–9; John Wahlke *et al.*, *The Legislative System: Explorations in Legislative Behavior*; and the articles contained in *Congress: Two Decades of Analysis*, ed. Ralph K. Huitt and Robert L. Peabody.

10 For the logic of such an approach, see Manley, "House Committee on Ways and Means: 1947–1966," pp. 5–9.

one former Senator, also a former minister of finance, twenty Senate staff members, one former Senate staff member, two Chamber staff members, officials in the executive branch and in the political parties); a detailed analysis of documents, committee reports, floor debates, and the work of other scholars; and extensive empirical observation of the operation of the Chilean Congress. Political parties will be abbreviated thusly: Partido Nacional, or National party (PN); Partido Radical, or Radical party (PR); Partido Demócrata Cristiano, or Christian-Democrat party (PDC); Vanguardia del Pueblo, or Vanguard of the People (VNP); Partido Democrático Nacional, or National Democrat party (PADENA); Partido Socialista, or Socialist party (PS); Partido Comunista, or Communist party (PC); Partido Conservador Unido, or United Conservative Party (PCU); and the Independiente, or Independents (I).

THE CHILEAN SENATE

INTERNAL DISTRIBUTION OF INFLUENCE

1. Decisional Role of the Senate in the Chilean Political System

SETTING

CHILE HAS A HIGHLY CENTRALIZED, unitary, quasi-presidential political system. The president has a fixed term (six years), and members of the cabinet are chosen by and are responsible to him, although Congress has the constitutional right to impeach ministers.[1]

NOTE: Portions of this chapter originally appeared in *Legislatures in Developmental Perspective*, ed. Allan Kornberg and Lloyd D. Musolf (Durham, N.C.: Duke University Press, 1970), and are used here in revised form with the permission of the publisher.

[1] Silvert prefers to describe the Chilean political system as "semiparliamentary" (Kalman H. Silvert, *Chile: Yesterday and Today*, p. 93) or "neoparliamentary" (Kalman H. Silvert, *The Conflict Society: Reaction and Revolution in Latin America*, p. 27), and Federico G. Gil uses the term "restricted parliamentary" (*The Political System of Chile*, p. 89). Their contention is that in a fully presidential system,

If the president selects a congressman for a cabinet post (usually a deputy and rarely a senator), the congressman must give up his seat. The Congress is bicameral—the Senate, currently numbering 45 members, and the Chamber of Deputies, 147.[2] The military has traditionally abstained from active participation in politics, "acting as a veto group only in so far as their own interests are concerned."[3] A proportional representation system is used for congressional elections in an effort to assure faithful representation of all shades of political opinion.

Although it is debatable how faithful representation is,[4] the electoral process has enabled Congress (especially the Senate) to serve as an effective opposition site. Robert Dix has characterized Chile (as well as Costa Rica and Uruguay) as follows: "The opposition role is substantially (though not definitively) legitimized. The presidency

---

cabinet ministers are the servants of only the president. In Chile, Congress may impeach ministers, who are answerable for their actions before Congress. It seems more accurate to describe the system as "quasi-presidential," in view of the way the system actually works. First, the president has a fixed six-year term, which cannot be cut short by a vote of no confidence. Congress has the constitutional prerogative to impeach the president under certain limited circumstances, but the prerogative has not been exercised in modern times. Second, although Congress also has the constitutional right to impeach ministers, the Chilean scholar Carlos Andrade Geywitz notes in *Elementos de derecho constitucional chileno* that such proceedings have seldom passed both houses. Finally, it is customary for ministers to explain their actions to Congress and even to participate in debates on key legislation. But this is not unlike the American system, where cabinet members appear before hearings on well-publicized congressional standing committees.

[2] The respective membership increased from 45 to 50 and from 147 to 150 as of the 1969 congressional elections.

[3] Silvert, *The Conflict Society*, p. 23. Witness the comment by General Sergio Castillo Aránguiz, chief of staff, at the Conference of American Armed Forces in Río: "The function of the armed forces should not be political, but rather to take advantage of modern technology to bring the country along the road of development, as occurs in Chile, where the armed forces enjoy much prestige" (*El Mercurio*, September 29, 1968, p. 33).

[4] The degree to which the system faithfully represents all shades of opinion is examined in a now dated work, Richard Cruz-Coke's *Geografía electoral de Chile*. The most recent accounts that touch on this, among other subjects, are Germán Urzua Valenzuela, *Los partidos políticos chilenos—las fuerzas políticas*, pp. 128–129, 148, 165, 175; and Carlos Andrade Geywitz, *Elementos de derecho constitucional chileno*, pp. 313–324.

has been won two or more times by the opposition during the 25-year period; the opposition wins over a third of the votes of the legislative seats in most elections; there have been no or only very brief (e.g., Costa Rica, 1948–49) periods of non-constitutional rule."[5]

"The result has been one of the most stable multiparty systems in Latin America,"[6] one that "has successfully evolved from an aristocratic oligarchic democracy into one in which the masses play the leading role."[7] Indeed, Flanigan and Fogleman's index of democratization for the period 1900–1950 places Chile fifth behind Canada, England, the United States, and Switzerland, and ahead of the important European nations of France, Italy, and Germany.[8]

"Chile is the only Latin American country where political forces are clearly and distinctly aligned, as in many European countries, into three great blocs: the Right, the Center, and the Left."[9] In the period of approximately one hundred years during which the multiparty system has functioned in Chile, the number of parties in existence has varied widely, reaching a maximum of thirty-six in 1953. Recently, five major parties have dominated the political field, ranging from right to left as follows: National, Radical, Christian-Democrat, Social-

[5] Robert H. Dix, "Oppositions and Development in Latin America" (Paper delivered at the 1967 Annual Meeting of the American Political Science Association, Chicago, September 5–9, 1967), p. 24. Note his other comments on Chile, especially pp. 6–9, 11 n. 11, 17, 26.

[6] Silvert, *The Conflict Society*, p. 27.

[7] Charles O. Porter and Robert J. Alexander, *The Struggle for Democracy in Latin America*, p. 6. For a Chilean interpretation of this evolution, see Julio Heise Gonzáles, *150 años de evolución institucional*.

[8] William Flanigan and Edwin Fogleman, "Patterns of Political Development and Democratization: A Quantitative Analysis" (Paper delivered at the 1967 Annual Meeting of the American Political Science Association, Chicago, September 5–9, 1967), fig. 6 between pp. 13 and 14. This index updated to 1968 would not alter this placement. An index of democratization is of course normative. I do not wish to imply in its use that political democracy—especially that modeled after the United States—necessarily equates with political development (i.e., "will and capacity to cope with and to generate continuing transformation toward whichever values seem appropriate in the particular context"). Nevertheless, it is one means (among others) by which valued goals may be achieved, and it is the system that has been adopted with appropriate Chileanization in this country. Therefore, when speaking of Chile, it is correct to make this equation.

[9] Gil, *Political System of Chile*, p. 244.

ist, and Communist. Ideologically, the Chilean political scale leans to the Left, with important factions in the two largest parties (Christian-Democrat and Radical) tending toward detentes with the Socialist and Communist parties.

Chile is also characterized by a Congress that exercises real influence in the political system. For example, Robert Scott notes that, although the legislatures in most of the countries of Latin America only go through the formal steps of lawmaking while their acts are in fact frequently dictated by presidents, in Chile "the center of power has virtually been transferred from the president to the legislature."[10] Numerous other American, Chilean, and Cuban scholars have presented specific examples of Congress's decisional voice, and selected statements from President Eduardo Frei's 1968 message to Congress provide still further evidence.[11]

Although these scholars would agree that Congress and particularly the Senate exercise important influence in the decision-making process, they probably also would contend that vis-à-vis one another, the executive has a more important role insofar as policy initiation is concerned.

---

[10] Robert E. Scott, "Legislatures and Legislation," in *Government and Politics in Latin America*, ed. Harold E. Davis, p. 331. For his other comments on Chile, see pp. 298–331 *passim*.

[11] For examples, see: William S. Stokes, "Parliamentary Government in Latin America," *American Political Science Review* 39, no. 3 (1945): p. 527; Silvert, *Chile: Yesterday and Today*, pp. 93, 191; Gil, *Political System of Chile*, pp. 117–118; Federico G. Gil and Charles J. Parrish, *The Chilean Presidential Election of September 4, 1964*, pt. 1, pp. 3, 5; Martin C. Needler, *Latin American Politics in Perspective*, p. 156; Albert O. Hirschman, *Journeys toward Progress: Studies of Economic Policy-Making in Latin America*, pp. 260, 268; Frederick M. Nunn, "Chile's Government in Perspective: Political Change or More of the Same?" *Inter-American Economic Affairs* 20, no. 4 (Spring, 1967): 83–84, 87–88; Charles J. Parrish, Arpad J. von Lazar, and Jorge Tapia Videla, *The Chilean Congressional Election of March 7, 1965: An Analysis*, pp. 27–28; Orville G. Cope, "The 1964 Presidential Election in Chile: The Politics of Change and Access," *Inter-American Economics Affairs* 20, no. 4 (Spring, 1967): 17 n. 25; Constantine C. Menges, "Public Policy and Organized Business in Chile: A Preliminary Analysis," *Journal of International Affairs* 20, no. 2 (1966): 354; Jorge A. Tapia Valdés, *La técnica legislativa*, pp. 40–41, 43; Ada I. Manríquez G., *El senado en Chile*, p. 164; *Cuatro mensaje del presidente de la república de Chile don Eduardo Frei Montalva al inaugurar el periodo de sesiones ordinarias del congreso nacional, 21 de mayo de 1968*, pp. 52, 74, 76–78.

They would base this contention on the president's considerable formal powers as outlined in the Constitution. For example, the president may classify certain legislation urgent, thereby setting a time limit in which Congress must pass the bill.[12] He also has "exclusive" areas of initiative—for example, in proposing the annual budget—and Congress is supposedly limited to reducing the requested expenditures of funds.[13] Congress may also grant extraordinary powers to the executive in emergency situations, and he has wide veto powers (e.g., item and additive).[14] It should be noted, however, that there has been little systematic empirical analysis to probe the degree to which Congress's influence is in fact restricted by these formal executive prerogatives.

If the Chilean Senate exercises real influence, an intensive study of the internal distribution of its influence is justified. And, despite the president's extraordinary urgency powers, the Senate does exercise considerable lawmaking initiative and can delay, modify, and defeat legislation generated by the executive. The Senate also oversees the bureaucracy, granting patronage, articulating interests, and resolving conflicts. To explain the bases of the Senate's rather extraordinary powers we will adopt, for comparative purposes, the outline for study of decisional function used by Robert Packenham in a recent survey of world legislatures: (1) lawmaking (initiation); (2) lawmaking (modification and delay); (3) administrative oversight and patronage; and (4) interest articulation and conflict resolution.[15]

---

[12] Gil, *Political System of Chile*, p. 103.

[13] For example, see Manuel Matus Benavente, *Desniveles entre presupuestos iniciales y presupuestos realizados*. In December, 1969, Congress passed several constitutional reforms that strengthened the president's hand still further. But, it is still too soon to tell whether the president will be as free to use these new prerogatives as the amended Constitution suggests. For more details, see "Texto completo del discurso del Presidente Frei," *El Mercurio*, December 31, 1969, p. 22; and "Congreso pleno aprobo reformas constitucionales," *El Mercurio*, December 30, 1969, pp. 1, 12, 22.

[14] "Constitución política de la república de Chile," in *Manual del senado*. The additive veto enables the president of the Republic to add totally new legislation to a bill; the item veto allows him to remove from a bill those pieces of legislation he does not like.

[15] Robert A. Packenham, "Legislatures and Political Development," which ap-

DECISIONAL FUNCTION

Lawmaking: Initiation

A close examination of the executive's urgency powers and the budgetary process indicates that Congress exercises far more initiative than scholars have previously suggested. First, let us consider the president's urgency powers. Since bills classified urgent by the president have priority on congressional calendars and must be discussed and dispatched within a specified time limit, it is often concluded that Congress has little opportunity to present its own legislation. But what has not been sufficiently stressed is that Congress is free to accept *or* reject the president's legislation. Since the executive normally lacks a sufficient majority in one of the two chambers to pass the bill (usually the Senate), congressmen use this lever to initiate numerous unrelated bills, in the form of amendments on its coattails. The president frequently agrees to tolerate many of them rather than have his proposed bill rejected within the required period.[16]

A recent example was the 1968 Salary Readjustment Bill, which President Frei tagged "as important as the annual budget."[17] Before final clearance by the Senate, it was the subject of more than two thousand attempted amendments, and many were new bills unrelated to the law in question.[18] Two senators and an important staff member observe:

These miscellaneous laws have the advantage of accelerating passage

---

pears in *Legislatures in Developmental Perspective*, ed. Allan Kornberg and Lloyd Musolf, pp. 521–582.

[16] Tapia Valdés, *La técnica legislativa*, pp. 41, 43–45. The constitutional reform passed in December, 1969, seeks to put an end to this process. It remains to be seen whether this can be achieved in a multiparty system that requires agreements and compromises in order to generate a majority large enough to pass important legislation.

[17] *Cuatro mensaje*, p. 76.

[18] *Indicaciones formuladas al proyecto de ley que reajuste las remuneraciones de los empleados y obreros de los sectores público y privado, para el año 1968*, Senate bull. no. 23519; based on standing committee reports, debates, interviews, and observations during this period. For an excellent service, see the photocopies of all newspaper accounts: "Cambios ministeriales," *Boletín de Información General* no. 37 (OIS).

—it is the only way some bills would get passed. There are many bills, perhaps, that shouldn't get passed, but they got tacked onto important legislation. The presidents of standing committees have the power to rule unconstitutional or extraneous to the material of the bill such amendments, but they often don't or can't use this power, depending on the situation.

The congressman must add on items of importance to him—it is the only way to get them passed, and the executive has to accept some of this. Presidents of standing committees do also—there is a certain amount of tolerance.

This process of amendments is worse than ever before, but it is a way of putting pressure on the president as well as of getting your own bills through.

As far as the annual budget is concerned, although Congress is restricted by the Constitution from directly increasing the annual budget, indirectly it is able to circumvent this restriction by passing laws during the year that entail permanent expenses and must be included in the annual budget according to Article 44, Section 4, of the Constitution.[19] Although Congress is not supposed to pass laws during the year that involve new expenses without at the same time indicating the source of financing, it escapes this shackle by simply indicating that the source of funds is a future annual budget.[20] Congress may also decrease variable budget expenses during the fiscal year. This power, when it chooses to exercise it, permits Congress to bargain with the executive.[21]

There is also abundant evidence that Congress influences the formulation of executive legislation prior to actual presentation. Cabinet ministers may try out several alternative proposals on party congressmen, not only for their personal reaction, but also to solicit their response as to what they sense Congress (especially the Senate opposition) will accept. Or the president and his cabinet may directly approach congressional leaders for their views on a particular bill.

[19] *El proceso presupuestario fiscal chileno*, p. 41.
[20] Arnaldo Gorziglia Balbi, *Facultades presupuestarias legislativas*, p. 124.
[21] *El proceso presupuestario*, p. 40. Although the constitutional reforms passed in December, 1969, also seek to limit this process, I am skeptical that this will be accomplished in practice.

One government (PDC) senator discussed these exchanges: "Sure, a minister may call the presidents of the respective parties [who are often senators], and have them over for an informal dinner one night . . ." The president himself indicated his frequent communication with Congress when urging constitutional reforms: "I can say that senators and deputies of the most distinct political viewpoints, in private conversations, have told me of their conviction that this situation [salary adjustment and unfinanced social security system] cannot continue and should be solved soon . . ."[22]

A tangible example of such activity involved the 1968 Salary Readjustment Bill. After Sergio Molina, minister of finance, resigned over the Senate's opposition to his proposal in January, 1968, Raúl Sáez replaced him.[23] Sáez began to explore possible alternative approaches with the leadership of opposition parties. Víctor García, president of the National party, declared, after talking with Sáez, "The Minister . . . has pointed out the need to discuss the general aspects of the project before it is sent to Congress . . . Sáez called us to know our opinion, and not to impose his point of view . . ."[24] Sáez himself was quoted as saying: "I think that if they have rejected the previous bill, they have proposals to make. I hope to hear them and see what can be done . . ."[25]

Lawmaking: Modification or Delay

The Senate also appears to be able to modify or delay the president's legislation. First of all, Article 138 of the Senate Reglamento (internal rules and procedures) prohibits the Senate or a standing committee from considering more than one urgency bill at the same time.[26] This provision obviously enables them to draw out the time period in which they consider executive-inspired urgency legislation. Second, the presi-

---

22 *Cuatro mensaje*, p. 77.

23 "Juró el nuevo gabinete," *El Mercurio*, February 16, 1968, p. 1.

24 "Positivo primer contacto de Sáez con dirigentes políticos," *El Mercurio*, February 23, 1968, p. 1.

25 "Función de la empresa privada destacan dos nuevos ministros," *El Mercurio*, February 24, 1968, p. 1.

26 "Reglamento del senado," in *Manual del senado*, p. 158.

dent's urgency prerogative is considerably weakened if he lacks a majority in either chamber. Congress will simply reject the proposed bill in the required time limit. Faced with this alternative, the president will either (1) withdraw and resubmit the bill several times, starting the urgency period over again from the beginning each time; (2) attempt to reach a compromise solution with the opposition; or (3) simply give Congress more time to consider it. He may even discard the bill altogether.[27]

Two examples illustrating this process are the bill on public housing developments and the 1968 University Reform Law. The Public Housing Development Bill was sent to the Senate standing committees of Public Works and Finance on September 7, 1965 (See Table 1). After the bill had been more than three months in committee, the president decided to ask for urgency classification, thereby requiring passage within thirty days. It became clear to the president two weeks later that the committees would report out the bill within the required time limit, but not in the form desired. Therefore, on January 12, 1966, the executive retired and immediately presented the same bill again, thereby starting the time limit all over from the beginning. By mid-July, this procedure had been repeated four times and over ten months had elapsed since original submission to the Senate.

In the case of the University Reform Law, the president arrived at a compromise solution with the Senate opposition, which allowed for rapid dispatch of the bill (60 days) but also provided more time for committee study than a simple urgency classification would have. Hence, in May, 1968, the floor leaders of the PC, PDC, PR, and PS (there are two for each party, called *comités*) issued this public statement:

The representatives declare that the project contains matters of great importance that require study and careful legislation. . . . The periods for a petition of urgency are insufficient to make such a study. . . . In view of this, we have asked the minister of education . . . to ask the president to retire the urgency . . . and we indicated that a period of sixty days was a

27 Andrade Geywitz, *Elementos de derecho constitucional chileno*, p. 439.

TABLE 1: Senate Delay of Public Housing Development Bill
Declared Urgent by President

Date	Session	Senate Action
9/7/65	43a	Bill sent to Senate committees of Public Works and Finance.
11/3/65	27a	Include bill in list of bills to be considered.
12/22/65	46a	Presents executive urgency request. Classified simple urgency.
1/4/66	52a	Agree to give committees extra week to review bill.
1/12/66	57a	Executive retires urgency and presents bill again. Classified simple urgency again.
1/25/66	67a	Executive retires urgency again.
5/31/66	1a	Executive presents urgency again for third time. Classified simple urgency.
7/7/66	3a	Time limit of 7/15 is given to Public Works Committee to report out the bill.
7/15/66	7a	Executive for the fourth time retires urgency.

SOURCE: Senate Office of Information Consultations, 1967 file.

prudent and legitimate period to study the initiative, obtain all the relevant data, and hear the opinions of the authorities of the universities.[28]

Except by special Senate agreement or executive urgency (and we have seen how effective this is in fact), a standing committee does not normally have a fixed period in which it must report out a bill.[29] Matters pending in Senate standing committees as of May, 1968, filled a sixty-page booklet.[30] Should the originating chamber reject a

[28] *Declaración de los comités comunista, demócrata christiano, radical y socialista del senado en relación con el estudio del proyecto que legisla sobre las universidades.*
[29] Tapia Valdés, *La técnica legislativa*, p. 28.
[30] *Senado—asuntos pendientes en comisiones al 21 de mayo de 1968.*

law, it may not be introduced again for another year.[31] On paper, the president's veto powers appear substantial (e.g., item, additive). But the fact that the executive normally lacks a majority to pass his legislation in both houses often forces him to make informal bargains with the opposition on how he will exercise his veto power once the bill leaves Congress. Furthermore, Congress may also overrule a presidential veto by a two-thirds vote of both houses, and the president cannot use his additive veto on matters of constitutional reform, as he can with a normal bill.[32]

Table 2 illustrates how the Senate delayed the dispatch of five additional key pieces of legislation during President Frei's administration. Note that standing committees of the Chilean Senate often are the central arena in the process. For example, of the total eighty-seven days required to pass the bill entitled Creation of a Committee to Adjust National Defense Pensions, eighty-five days (98%) were spent in committee. Frequently, it is in committee that bills are carefully studied and most compromises pounded out. "Without public tribunes, official versions, and so on, there is more calm; it is much easier to produce a climate that leads to agreement on different points of view. There is less passion, and more give and take when an idea has merit."[33]

Delay should not be considered as necessarily negative in effect. There is considerable evidence that the Senate improves the laws it modifies or delays, which reflects a serious and professional standing committee analysis, comparable with that of U.S. Senate committees.[34] Those who regard Senate delays or modifications as undue harassment of a government that currently leans to the Left should not forget that the Senate has acted no differently when the president represented the Right. Examine these excerpts from Senate debates, for example:

---

[31] Adela Ramos Pazos, *La función legislativa*, p. 32.

[32] Andrade Geywitz, *Elementos de derecho constitucional chileno*, p. 650. See also Alejandro Silva Bascuñán, *Tratado de derecho constitucional*, III, 493.

[33] Andrade Geywitz, *Elementos de derecho constitucional chileno*, p. 446.

[34] Tapia Valdés, *La técnica legislativa*, p. 31; Guillermo Bruna Contreras, *Estatuto de la profesión parlamentaria*, p. 8. The relative autonomy of standing committees from national political party leadership will be examined later.

TABLE 2: Senate Time Taken to Pass Five Key Administrative Bills

Title of Bill	Time in Committee		Time on Floor		Total Time in Senate	
	%	Days	%	Days	%	Days
1. Creation of a Committee to Adjust National Defense Pensions	98	85	2	2	100	87
2. Creation of New Ministry of Housing and Urbanization	97	131	3	4	100	135
3. Exemption of Property from Tax if Valued Less Than E 5,000	86	101	14	17	100	118
4. Rules to Stimulate Exports	84	84	16	16	100	100
5. Creation of a Director of National Boundaries and Frontiers	49	97	51	98	100	195

SOURCE: Senate Office of Information Consultations, 1967 file.

Altamirano [PS]: No other president had his initiatives approved in block. . . . The government says that all of its predecessors were given extraordinary faculties. This is a half truth. . . . During the last administration of Mr. Ibáñez, he was not given faculties to restructure either the Central Bank or the controller general's office. And, if I remember correctly, Senator Enríquez, who is also president of the Radical Party, demanded substantial modifications of the faculties asked by former President Jorge Alessandri. . . .

Aguirre Doolan [PR]: For example, faculties to legislate over social security and the petroleum industry were not given.[35]

Administrative Oversight and Patronage

Effective legislative scrutiny of administrative performance must be based in part on the capacity to obtain necessary information (particu-

[35] *Diario de sesiones del senado, legislatura extraordinaria*, sesión 87a, February 23, 1967, p. 4306.

larly executive agency documents), and an adequate staff to seek out and analyze this data.

Passage of Article 5 of Law 13.609 in 1959 gave the Senate both the authority and staff to perform this function more energetically.[36] First of all, the Office of Information of the Senate (OIS) was created. Composed of economists, political scientists and public administrators, lawyers, translators, and a newspaperman, OIS conducts valuable studies on the performance of administrative agencies for senators. Second, Law 13.609, tested and upheld in several legal cases over a period of eight years, requires all administrative agencies to forward whatever information or data OIS deems necessary to complete these studies.

Let us take a recent test case. In 1968, OIS sought to evaluate the progress of Chilean agrarian reform from 1964 to 1968. OIS asked the Agrarian Reform Corporation (Corporación de la Reforma Agraria, or CORA) to submit the balances of agriculture settlements (*asentamientos*) for this purpose. After some resistance by CORA, the controller general ruled on July 6, 1968, that the information must be provided, as in the past, and it subsequently was.[37]

Legislative control of administrative performance is frequently weakened because opposition senators do not have access to executive documents they need. In Chile, this does not appear to be true for the Senate. The fact that OIS conducts studies for all senators in a non-partisan manner is, in effect, an institutionalized guarantee of information for the opposition. An analysis of OIS *consultas* (studies or consultations) for the period 1967–1968 (March), reveals that 91 percent (329) of the total 363 consultations were in answer to requests made by opposition senators (see Table 3).

Subject matter standing committee hearings and floor debates are also used by the Senate to review administrative activity. For example,

---

[36] "Disposiciones legales y labor que desarrolla la oficina de informaciones del senado," *Boletín de información general* no. 18.

[37] For a more detailed account, see the author's "Senate vs. CORA: An Attempt to Evaluate Chile's Agrarian Reform to Date," *Inter-American Economic Affairs* 22 (Autumn, 1968): 47–53, and a shorter version in Land Tenure Center (Univ. of Wisconsin) no. 2 (March–August, 1968), pp. 1–7.

TABLE 3: OIS Consultations, 1967–1968: Ordinary Sessions

			Party Requesting Consultation					
	PC	PS	PADENA	PDC	I	PR	PN	Total
	N	N	N	N	N	N	N	N
1967	109	89	1	28	14	30	14	285
1968	32	19	1	6	2	17	1	78
Total	141=39%	108=30%	2=1%	34=9%	16=4%	47=13%	15=4%	363=100%

SOURCE: Senate Office of Information Consultations.
NOTE: Coverage does not include consultations to committee secretaries or other personnel. 1968 is to March 31, 1968.

interviews and extensive personal observation show that ministries regularly appear before Senate committees to explain both policy stands and bureaucratic performance. On the floor, senators often call attention to administrative bottlenecks by taking advantage of the *hora de incidentes* (hour of incidental matters). During this period, senators can bring up or debate whatever matters they deem to be in the public interest.

In particular instances, committee hearings and floor debates may lead Congress to request that the controller general conduct an audit of an administrative program to determine whether funds have been spent as Congress intended. Or a committee may travel to an agrarian reform settlement, for example, to verify the information provided by the Agrarian Reform Corporation. The Chamber may also set up special investigating committees to explore a particular matter. Furthermore, if the evidence warrants such action, the Chamber can and sometimes does start impeachment proceedings against a minister. If the measure passes the Chamber, the Senate must make the final decision. As Table 4 indicates, the Senate as a rule votes not to impeach, but, if sufficiently provoked or justified, it will vote otherwise, as happened on several occasions during the Ibáñez administration (1952–1958). The same is true for local officials (mayors, for example). Finally, the Senate may also seek to alter administration policies (or their implementation) by refusing to approve military

TABLE 4: Impeachment Proceedings in Congress, 1926–1966

Year	No. of Accusations	Chamber Approved	Senate Approved[a]
1926–27	1	—	0
1931	9	6	1
1935	2	—	0
1936	2	—	0
1938	2	—	0
1939	2	1	—
1940	3	2	1
1944	1	—	0
1945	1	1	1
1946	1	—	0
1947	1	—	0
1948	1	—	0
1951	1	—	0
1952	1	—	0
1954	1	—	0
1955	1	1	0
1956	1	—	0
1957	3	2	1
1958	1	—	0
1959	1	—	0
1960	4	—	0
1962	1	—	0
1963	2	—	0
1966	2	—	0
Total	49	13 = 27%	4 = 8%

SOURCE: Senate Office of Information Consultations, 1967 file.

[a] Zero indicates that the Senate did not consider the case, since the Chamber itself rejected the charges.

advancements, diplomatic appointments, and presidential travels abroad, as occurred on two occasions in 1967 and 1968.[38]

As we saw earlier, the Senate exercises some control over financial resources and therefore has an instrument, patronage, by which to

[38] We discussed earlier Senate refusal to allow Frei to travel to the United States in 1967. The Senate also rejected a diplomatic appointment to Peru in 1968.

exert influence. Friends and constituents regularly approach senators for political appointments or other special favors. Reviewing his mail, one senator cited a typical group of solicitations: "Here is a woman who wants me to get her a naval pension because her husband died recently. Another is a man who wants me to get him a job as an elevator operator." Jorge Tapia Valdés points out that 55.2 percent of the laws passed by Congress between 1938 and 1958 were over such particular matters as pensions, jobs, or retirement benefits (*asuntos de gracia*) in response to these requests.[39]

Interest Articulation and Conflict Resolution

Congress not only articulates interests but also resolves conflicts, in part by initiating or modifying legislation in response to demands made upon it. This action takes place on three levels—particular (groups or individuals), provincial (*agrupación*), and national.

Pressure groups have a long history in Chile (e.g., the National Society of Agriculture was formed in 1838) and, unlike Brazil, for example, they have close contact with Congress. Constantine Menges writes:

Chile's business associations have the usual types of formal access to the legislature. They may testify on bills before appropriate committees, and they submit documentation stating their views on legislation under discussion. Each of the major peak organizations keeps a close watch over the legislative calendar and informs potentially interested members of developments. The peak organizations also very often serve as middlemen in transmitting the views of member associations and individual companies to the Congress. . . .

Following the pattern of American business group activity, however, it seems that the really important contact with the legislature involves informal relations with individual congressmen. . . . In the case of controversial legislation, business association leaders present their views and perhaps even coordinate strategy with sympathetic congressmen.[40]

Menges also notes that parliamentary groups of some of the major political parties may effectively make policy on some or all issues in

[39] Tapia Valdés, *La técnica legislativa*, p. 47.
[40] Menges, "Public Policy and Organized Business in Chile," p. 354.

Chile, just as Robert MacKenzie found in England. If this is the case, "Contact of business association leaders and prominent individual congressmen would be tantamount to contact with a party organization rather than a free agent."[41]

But, if the business community has its linkage with Congress, so does the Left. There are at present six PS and five PC senators (not counting independents or small parties tied to this group) of a total forty-five senators. One PC senator was formerly director of the party paper, *El Siglo*, and two others were former union directors; they view their role as representing the worker and marginal groups. Data indicate that, just as the Right attempts to chair the standing committees of Finance or Economy and Commerce, the Left shows interest in Labor and Social Legislation or Public Health (see chapter 4). Colonization of the presidencies of different committees and ties with individual congressmen insure access to competing interests, "permitting a balance of forces, more facts, and resolution with greater clarity."[42]

Before 1925, senators were elected by provincial assemblies, and they thought of themselves as representing regional and local interests. President Alessandri Palma attempted to make the Senate less provincial and more national in outlook but was forced to accept a compromise solution whereby senators are now elected by a group of provinces (*agrupación*) directly by the people. As in the United States, a fixed number of senators represent each *agrupación*, maintain frequent contact with their constituency, and have on occasion voted against their party in preference to regional interests. "Pork" committees like Public Works and Government are popular among senators because they control funds for roads and water, which directly involve the electoral interests of each congressman.

Many senators find regional election and representation a useful mechanism for reconciling conflict between societal and regional interests. One senator argues: ". . . in my view ⌈it⌉ is the escape valve

---

41 *Ibid.*

42 Tapia Valdés, *La técnica legislativa*, p. 41. For a description of the place of this structure in conflict management, see Malcolm E. Jewell and Samuel C. Patterson, *The Legislative Process in the United States*, p. 11.

[*válvula de escape*] that preserves our system. With our unitary system, which tends toward control from Santiago, and, at the same time, regions with such diverse characteristics and needs, direct representation by *agrupación* is necessary." But many senators do not share this view. They find "errand-boy" tasks distasteful and concern for re-election degrading; they prefer to see the Senate as representing the national interest, at times as a brake (*freno*) on the Chamber. They contend that the objective of partial election of senators is to encourage a national versus a regional view on issues, and certain senators would favor disallowing re-election for this purpose. Some of this latter group of senators find re-election difficult, and others gravitate to "safe" districts. But some are reelected consistently because they so admirably perform this role. Therein lies the importance of the *form* the Senate functions of interest articulation and conflict resolution take. It is the meshing of each level—individual or group, region, and nation—that aids national integration and persistence of the political system. One senator sums it up nicely:

> On the one hand is the problem of national disintegration. . . . Each region tries to obtain privileges, principally on taxes. . . . This tendency is seen primarily in the frontier zones, and, at times, one hears talk of total separation. Some see a national role orientation as a response to this problem. On the other hand, there is the question of centralism [in capital and geographically]—a trend considered adverse to our development. If you create a national senator, this process would be accentuated. The conclusion has always been that the existing system is the best overall solution to both problems.

BASIS FOR DECISIONAL INFLUENCE

Several factors help explain the Senate's considerable influence in the political system. The first is the long historical development of the institution.[43] At first (1812), the Senate was little more than a legitimating body, and its members were selected by the executive. But by 1818 disagreements began to arise between the two powers when President O'Higgins sought to exercise prerogatives not granted

---

[43] Luis E. Williamson Jordan, *La evolución del senado en Chile*, p. 21.

him in the formal constitution; President O'Higgins decided to dissolve the body in 1822.

After several subsequent changes, a Senate was set up under the Constitution of 1833 that was to last until 1874. The first seeds of increasing decisional power were planted here, when member selection was formally shifted from the president to provincial assemblies and later, in 1874, to the public. Although the objective of the 1833 constitution was "to establish a strong executive independent of the pressure and tyranny of parliament,"[44] Manuel Antonio Tocornal returned from European travels in 1848 with a new concept of Congress's role. His ideas subsequently led to even greater influence for Congress with a corresponding decrease in the relative importance of its legitimating role. This movement culminated in the "revolution" of 1891 with the establishment of a parliamentary regime that was to last until 1925.

On balance, despite all the bad effects generally attributed to this period, it should also be recognized that "it facilitated the development of new social groups: the middle class and the proletariat. Also, it made possible the organization of popular political parties: Workers, Socialist, and Communist. . . . In this manner, the parliamentary period was a magnificent civic school for the Chilean people."[45] Functionally and institutionally, presidential veto power was modified, the need for Senate approval of diplomatic appointments established, and ethical guidelines for member activities outside Congress defined.

The evolutionary trend toward greater congressional influence proved difficult to reverse or overcome in 1924, when attempts were made to re-establish presidential pre-eminence. Many of President Alessandri Palma's proposals for stronger executive power (for example, the right to dissolve Congress) were rejected by the Constitutional Committee that helped write the Constitution of 1925 (many

---

[44] "Versión oficial de la conferencia dictada por S. E. el presidente de la república, Arturo Alessandri Palma, en el Salón de Honor, de la Universidad de Chile, el dia viernes, 3 de Julio, 1925," which appears in *Actas oficiales de las sesiones celebradas por la comisión y subcomisiones encargadas del estudio del proyecto de nueva constitución política de la república*, p. 689.

[45] Heise González, *150 años de evolución institucional*, pp. 81–82.

members of which were congressmen).[46] Some congressional members
of the committee (PR, PCU, PC) actually presented simultaneously
to the public an alternative plan, which called for substantially less
change than the reform actually adopted.[47] Even after the new constitution was passed, effective reduction of Congress's decisional role
was limited by the number of congressmen who continued to serve
in 1926 as in 1924, carrying with them parliamentary traditions and
habits that reinforced the persistence of the Congress. As Table 5
indicates, twenty-seven (60%) of the forty-five senators elected in
1926 had been members of Congress in 1924, and this helps explain
the Senate's influence today.[48]

We have already touched on a second variable that gives Congress
such a strong voice in lawmaking—the presence of an opposition
majority in one of the two chambers. The traditional existence of such
a majority is in turn a product of several factors: (1) Congress is
elected in a different year than the president; (2) the Senate is only
partially renovated, and in such a way that it is difficult to win a
majority; (3) the president himself rarely wins more than a plurality
(Frei is an exception) and cannot run for another term; and (4)
even when a president obtains a majority, many voters give their
support only to prevent a less desirable candidate from being elected.
Under these circumstances, the next congressional election is viewed
as a more accurate reflection of the president's real support.[49]

Public opinion provides a third base in support of Congress's demands for a powerful voice in the policy process. In January, 1965,
Eduardo Hamuy asked a random sample of Santiago residents (just
after Frei's presidential election and before the March, 1965, congressional election—a time when the President's support was probably

---

[46] "Sesiones de la subcomisión de reformas constitucionales," in *Actas oficiales*,
pp. 382–388; see p. 5 for list of members of the first session of La Comisión Con-
sultiva, which added members later also.

[47] "Fórmula disidente," in *Actas oficiales*, pp. 644–646.

[48] Examine José Guillermo Guerra's *La constitución de 1925*, written in 1929
after constitutional reform, especially pp. 192–194.

[49] For example, President Frei obtained a majority of the popular votes in the
1964 presidential election. But many voters supported him only in preference to
Socialist candidate Salvador Allende.

TABLE 5: Congressional Carryover, Pre (1924) to Post (1926)
Constitutional Reform (1925)

| | 1926 Congress | | |
	Chamber	Senate[a]	Congress
Carryover	37 = 28%	27 = 60%	64 = 36%
Total	132	45	137

[a] Of the twenty-seven senator carryover, fourteen were deputies in 1924 who moved up to the Senate, and thirteen were senators in 1924, as in 1926.

at its apex): "Returning to the subject of the actual government, let us suppose that Frei cannot govern, because Congress obstructs his work. Would you be in favor of dissolving Congress so that the government could complete its program, or would you be in favor of waiting until the parliamentary elections of 1969 in order to obtain a favorable Congress?" Although 67.1 percent of the sample recognized that a conflict existed between the president and Congress and 73 percent felt that the president was correct versus 12 percent for Congress (based on other questions in the survey), only 36.8 percent favored dissolving Congress as the solution, 44.9 percent preferred to wait until the 1969 congressional elections, and only 1.3 percent favored a plebiscite (see Table 6). Even when social class is controlled, the variation in attitudes is relatively similar. Although the vast majority in this sample supported the president in this conflict and at this point in time, the majority were *not* prepared to undercut Congress's constitutionally guaranteed decision-making role by opting for dissolution or a plebiscite.

The public's reluctance to support dissolution may be due, in part, to Congress's demonstrated capacity to change. One measure of change is the career background of the Senate membership in 1965 versus 1933 (see Table 7). In 1933, ten (22%) of the senators were either former military men or rural representatives. But in 1965 this representation had dropped to two (4.5%) in response to greater urbanization, reduction of corrupt electoral practices, and civilian predominance in political life. Correspondingly, career backgrounds of

TABLE 6: Santiago Survey Sample: President Frei vs. Congress (January, 1965)

Alternatives	No.	%
Dissolve Congress	205	36.8
Wait until 1969 elections	250	44.9
President sign	18	3.2
Plebiscite	7	1.3
Unite, combine w/o parties	4	0.7
Pressure Congress	—	—
Other, or response in error	16	2.9
Not know, not answer	57	10.2
Total	557	100.0

SOURCE: These data were generously provided by Eduardo Hamuy from his January, 1965, print-out sheets, question 6Y, Universidad de Chile, Facultad de Ciencias Económicas-Centro de Estudias Socio-Económico's study.

senators totaled fifteen different types in 1965, versus eleven in 1933, and represented a wider spectrum, reflecting Chile's economic and political development during this period.

Nelson Polsby has argued that a political system is better able to make decisions authoritatively if it is institutionalized.[50] Hence, member stability and informal norms of Chamber-Senate apprenticeship provide the Chilean Senate with a fourth base of influence. Table 8 shows that of forty-five present (1968) members, thirty-one have served previously in the Chamber (eighteen of twenty-five in 1961, thirteen of twenty in 1965 or after). Of those originally elected in 1961 and 1965, thirty-five (78%) were deputies before, and only three senators have renounced to accept other positions (presidencies, ambassadorships to the United States and Argentina). This pattern has existed for more than thirty-five years (see Table 9).

Not only do a high percentage of the 1968 senators have previous Chamber experience, but they also frequently represent the *same* district repeatedly while in the Chamber. Their Chamber district often

[50] Nelson W. Polsby, "The Institutionalization of the U.S. House of Representatives," *American Political Science Review* 62 (March, 1968): 144.

TABLE 7: Senate Members' Career Background 1965–1969 vs. 1933–1937

Occupation	1933–1937 Senate		1965–1969 Senate	
	N	%	N	%
Lawyer	21	46.8	21	46.3
Doctor	2	4.6	2	4.4
Businessman	4	9.0	3	6.8
Civil engineer	—	—	2	4.5
Newspaperman	—	—	1	2.2
Worker	3	6.6	2	4.5
Chemical engineer	—	—	1	2.2
Accountant	—	—	2	4.5
Engineer	2	4.4	—	—
Agronomy engineer	—	—	1	2.2
Professor	—	—	2	4.5
Agriculturist	6	13.2	2	4.5
Ex-military	2	4.4	—	—
Writer	—	—	1	2.2
Industrialist	1	2.2	3	6.8
Winemaker	2	4.4	—	—
Architect	—	—	1	2.2
Ex-policeman	1	2.2	—	—
No data	1	2.2	1	2.2
Total	45	100.0	45	100.0

SOURCE: Senate Office of Information Consultations, 1966 file.
NOTE: Percentages have been slightly rounded to equal 100.0%.

TABLE 8: 1968 Senators with Prior Service in the Chamber of Deputies

Term	PC	PS	PADENA	PDC	VNP	I	PR	PN	Total
1961–1969	3	2	—	1	1	1	6	4	18
1965–1973	2	1	—	7	—	—	3	—	13
Total	5	3	—	8	1	1	9	4	31

SOURCE: Compiled from Library of Congress Biographical Data Project Files.

TABLE 9: Institutionalization of Congress

	Chamber							Senate					
Term	Total No.		FC[a]		AAP[b]		Term	Total No.		FC[a]		AAP[b]	
	%	N	%	N	%	N		%	N	%	N	%	N
1930–32	100	141	33	47	4	5	1933–37	100	27	41	11	4	1
1933–37	100	145	25	36	3	4[c]	1933–41	100	27	71	19	7	2
1937–41	100	156	46	71	5	8	1937–45	100	28	71	20	7	2
1941–45	100	150	46	69	2	3	1941–49	100	22	68	15	—	—
1945–49	100	150	60	90	1	1	1945–53	100	29	83	24	3	1[d]
1949–53	100	152	51	77	1	1[c]	1949–57	100	23	74	17	4	1[d]
1953–57	100	147	39	58	1	1	1953–61	100	25	60	15	—	—
1957–61	100	147	54	79	—	—	1957–65	100	21	72	15	5	1[d]
1961–65	100	148	59	88	—	—	1961–69	100	25	84[e]	21	—	—

SOURCE: Compiled from data in Guillermo Bruna Contreras, *Estatuto de la profesión parlamentaria*, pp. 19–25.

NOTE: Different numbers correspond to change in number of members over time, and to deaths, which cause other by-elections.

[a] Former congressmen.

[b] Accepted another post.

[c] Became senator in mid-term.

[d] Became president of Chile.

[e] This pattern continued in the March, 1969, congressional election. Eighty-three percent of the thirty Senators elected in 1969 (twenty-five) had either been deputies or senators before election.

forms a part of their *agrupación* once in the Senate, and they generally continue to represent it there. Thus we find a pattern similar to that of the United States. Thirty-four of the thirty-five senators who previously served in the Chamber represented the *same* district *all* during their period there. For twenty-six (74%), their Chamber district formed a part of the *same agrupación* they represented once in the Senate. The most typical Chamber-Senate career (see Table 10) totals nineteen years (nine in the Chamber, ten in the Senate), and a mean for the total 1968 Senate sample is seventeen years (see Table 11). This Chamber apprenticeship and district stability enables the senator to acquire knowledge, skills, and local contacts necessary for an influential legislative career.

TABLE 10: Typical Congressional Careers, 1968 Senate

Name	Chamber Prov.	Yrs.	Senate Agrup.	Yrs.	Total Yrs.
National party					
Bulnes	10a	8	5a	16	24
Curti	17a	8	7a	16	24
Radical party					
Bossay	6a	10	3a	16	26
Miranda[a]	4a	16	2a	8	24
Durán	21a	12	8a	16	28
Juliet	11a	20	6a	8	28
Enríquez	17a	12	7a	8	20
Independent					
Sepúlveda	23a	12	9a	8	20
Von Mühlenbrock	24a	8	9a	8	16
Natl. Vang. People					
Castro	9a	8	5a	8	16
Christian-Democrats					
Reyes	7a	16	4a	8	24
Palma	22a	8	2a	8	16
Musalem	7a	12	4a	8	20
Fuentealba[a]	4a	8	8a	8	16
Gumucio	7a	8	4a	8	16
Pablo	17a	4	7a	8	12
Socialist party					
Rodríquez	7a	4	9a	16	20
Altamirano	22a	4	4a	8	12
S. Corbalán[b]	17a	8	5a	6	14
Communist party					
Teitelboim	6a	4	4a	8	12
Campusano	7a	4	2a	8	12
Avg. career total		9		10	19

[a] Also president or secretary-general of his party.
[b] Died in 1967 and replaced by wife in off-year election.

TABLE 11: Length of Congressional Career Senate

Year Elected	PN	PR	MNI	AGL	Party UNI	I	PDC	PADENA	VNP	PS	PC	Total
1953												
No.	9	4	2	4	1	—	—	1	—	4	—	25
Yrs.	25	15	8	9	8	—	—	13	—	16	—	17
1957												
No.	8	5	—	3	—	—	1	—	—	3	—	20
Yrs.	18	28	—	12	—	—	15	—	—	9	—	19
1961												
No.	6	6	—	—	—	3	2	—	1	4	3	25
Yrs.	22	22	—	—	—	15	14	—	16	20	14	19[a]
1965												
No.	—	3	—	—	—	1	11	1	—	2	2	20
Yrs.	—	24	—	—	—	16	15	8	—	10	12	15[a]

NOTE: Abbreviations not noted elsewhere are:
MNI—National Movement for Ibáñez
AGL—Agrarian Labor
UNI—Independent National Union
[a] Mean career for 1961–1965 is 17.

The Senate's capacity for a lawmaking role is further enhanced by the support of a highly competent staff (see Table 12), which compares favorably with the staff available to the U.S. Congress.[51] Senators Exequiel González Madariaga (PR) and Baltazar Castro (VNP) give testimony to their reliance on the Senate staff:

> The Senate knows how much we value the collaboration of all the staff of the Senate, because they are our greatest allies in the legislative action that Congress achieves. Practically nothing can be done without the aid of all the personnel of the secretary . . . their collaboration through their experience, which has been acquired over a long period of work, at times leads us to a common solution . . .[52]

> We have always maintained that it is the staff of Congress . . . to a great extent that carries on the democratic tradition . . . they are the ones who show the way to those deputies and senators who arrive for the first time to Congress . . . on their stability and good judgment depends to a great extent the efficiency and capacity to work of Congress.[53]

Except for personal secretaries, the Senate staff is filled through competitive public examinations. Advancement is based on demonstrated ability and a long period of apprenticeship (*escalafón*).[54] Two of the most important components of the Senate staff are the standing committee secretaries and the Office of Information (OIS). Standing committee secretaries are an important driving force in a system where the principal work is done in committees. They are the ones who really study the laws and help inform the senators of their contents. They generally serve on the same committee for years, acquiring a high level of expertise and specialization in their committee's subject mat-

---

[51] Numerically, the Senate staff is modest by U.S. standards. But, when appropriate adjustments are made for the fact that Chile has only nine million people versus two hundred million in the United States, and that legislation is not as complex as in the more highly industrialized U.S. system, the proportionate impact of each staff member may be equal to or even greater than that for a staff member in the U.S. Senate.

[52] *Diario de sesiones del senado, legislativa extraordinaria*, sesión 12a, November 9, 1960, p. 643.

[53] *Diario de sesiones del senado, legislativa extraordinaria*, sesión 22a, December 6, 1961, p. 1009.

[54] Tapia Valdés, *La técnica legislativa*, pp. 32–33.

TABLE 12: Senate Staff Excluding Senators' Personal Secretaries, 1967

Position	Men	Women	Total
Personnel of Secy. of Senate	23	—	23
Office of Information	6	3	9
Editing personnel	19	2	21
Treasurer	2	—	2
General aide	1	—	1
Auxiliary services	1	5	6
Service aides	56	—	56
Dining room	14	—	14
Other positions	2	6	8
Contracted personnel	3	2	5
Building	28	4	32
Chefs	2	—	2
Total	157	23	179

SOURCE: Senate Office of Information Consultations, 1967 file.

ter. One senator exclaims: "The secretaries are extremely important. They are highly efficient and are the product of many years of experience in the Senate . . . they are the tradition of the Senate. I ask my friends—that is how we regard them—for their opinion on a project. That doesn't bother me at all. After all, many were in the same law classes, and we have been friends for years."

A typical career is that of Jorge A. Tapia Valdés, secretary of Constitution, Legislation, and Justice. Graduating in law in 1960, and author of the book, *La técnica legislativa*, Tapia began in the Senate in 1954. After more than twelve years of apprenticeship, he became the secretary of his committee.[55] Similarly, Rafael Eyzaguirre Echeverría received his law degree in 1947, became a secretary of Constitution, Legislation, and Justice after eighteen years in 1962, and presently is working on the Special Committee on Constitutional Reform. Eyzaguirre is also a professor of constitutional law at the University of Chile.[56]

[55] *Diccionario biográfico de Chile*, p. 1533.
[56] *Ibid.*, p. 484.

The secretaries and their aides are supplemented by the OIS. Also chosen by competitive examination, OIS carries out valuable in-depth studies for senators and secretaries of standing committees in a totally nonpartisan manner, as well as publishing numerous bulletins of information for the public media[57] (see Table 13).

The Senate staff demonstrates a high degree of adaptability to the periodic increase and decrease of demands made on it. As a rule, secretaries and their aides work on only one or two standing committees. But some committees work more than others, and some hardly at all. Therefore, in times of stress (e.g., 1968 Salary Readjustment Bill) or in the absence of a secretary, a temporary shift of secretaries or aides will take place to augment the capacity of a committee (e.g., Finance). Work hours follow a similar cycle, increasing in response to demands made on the system. Standing committees can and do call on experts for testimony and assessment. Senators also have a personal staff, but it is modest by U.S. standards (this varies by senator). This staff shortage is overcome in part by calling on party experts to help keep them informed on important bills.[58]

The existence of member stability, staff support, and norms that encourage work and specialization contrasts sharply with most other Latin American legislatures (see Table 14). For example, James Payne's data on the Colombian Congress show that member stability is low.[59] Regular members can be and are replaced by alternates, and only 25 percent return for a consecutive term (versus 78% for the Chilean Senate). Absenteeism is high. Committees seldom meet, and closed door sessions are rare (normal for the Chilean Senate). Colombian legislators are virtually without research or technical assistance and have no personal offices or secretaries (Chilean senators do).

A senator's personal ties (economic and kinship) and past experience should not be underestimated as a fifth source of lawmaking influence. Although it has been the subject of frequent debate, it is still quite legal for a congressman to be a director of a private com-

[57] "Disposiciones legales y labor," *Boletín de Información General* no. 18.

[58] See chapter 2 for a discussion of the relationship between senators and their respective national party leadership.

[59] See chapter 11 of James L. Payne, *Patterns of Conflict in Colombia.*

TABLE 13: OIS Work, 1964–1968

Type of Work	1964	1965	1966	1967	1967–68 Ext.[a]	1968 Reg.[a]
Consultations						
Sent out	740	1,017	1,049	967	621	318
Reports received	158	288	356	316	204	126
Requests for information						
Sent out	116	342	302	307	211	126
Received	165	125	261	244	271	166
Bulletins published						
Press information	29	13	6	—	1	6
Parliamentary information	40	52	45	57	65	40
Translations	34	29	34	65	71	17
Economic reports	10	17	22	28	23	11
General information	2	—	1	20	12	4
Statistical information	3	4	4	3	2	1
Documents loaned	375	525	461	355	252	232
Total communications sent	1,885	2,311	1,834	1,572	1,273	974
Total communications received	1,983	—	2,217	1,835	1,040	593
Messages	217	—	201	270	223	76
From Chamber	1,165	—	390	731	217	176
From ministries	433	—	954	536	414	239
From controller *et al.*	26	—	136	113	94	63
Requests of concern	81	—	74	48	11	18
Other contacts	61	—	462	137	81	21

SOURCE: Senate Office of Information (compiled from Annual Work Reports).

[a] Regular and extraordinary sessions. For idea of trend, combine last two (some overlap with 1967).

pany or bank as long as it does not have contract direct with the State[60] If a congressman is *at the same time* a director in an important private company or bank, a potentially powerful connection between public

[60] See Guillermo Guerra, *La constitución de 1925*, pp. 188–196, for his views in 1924 and 1929; and Manríquez G., *El senado en Chile*, p. 176, for a 1965 position. The PDC had as part of its constitutional reform project (passed by the Chamber and, as of early 1971, still in committee in the Senate) taken a position against the continuation of this linkage—if it ever passes, some of its own members will have to order their personal affairs.

TABLE 14: Comparison of Chilean Senate and Colombian Congress

Indicators of Institutionalization	Colombian Congress	Chilean Senate
Committees make policy	No	Yes
Congressmen have own staff and office	No	Yes
Research and technical staff	No	OIS, committee staff
System of alternates	Yes	No
Regular members attend sessions regularly	No	Yes (63%)
Percentage who return for consecutive term	25%	78%
Specialized knowledge or competence	No	Yes
Norms to facilitate policy-making (courtesy, deference, specialization)	No	Yes
Members concerned about policy output	No	Yes

SOURCE: Chilean Senate files and chapter 11 of Payne, *Patterns of Conflict in Colombia.*

and private careers is created that may be useful in initiating or modifying proposed legislation. Furthermore, if a congressman, through service in the executive branch, has acquired knowledge in the ins and outs of a ministry, personal loyalties, or expertise, a similar base is created.

Our study of the directors and top ten stockholders of the top 200 industrial firms (*sociedades anónimas*), top 25 insurance companies, and all domestic banks at the end of 1966, shows clearly that career overlap exists.[61] First, it is necessary to make clear the importance of

[61] Raw data were provided by the Superintendencia de Compañías de Seguros, Sociedades Anónimas y Bolsas de Comercio, and by the Superintendencia del Bancos for their most recent complete files.

the group we are talking about. For example, the top ten stockholders of the top 193 *sociedades anónimas* (7 are foreign), or 0.3 percent of all *sociedades anónimas* stockholders, own 62.3 percent of all *sociedades anónimas* value (*valor patrimonial*). Of the total number of directors of the top 193, 28 per cent are also stockholders in these companies, which represents a personal ownership of 6.4 percent of the value of all *sociedades anónimas*. If a person is a director or director-stockholder in one of these top 193 companies, he is a potentially influential individual in the economic community. If he is also horizontally linked to such institutions as the top insurance companies and banks, this potential is still greater. It is further increased if one is also such in more than one of this top group. Add to this the position of congressman *at the same time*, and an immense potential for influence is created. It is multiplied still further if the congressman also happens to sit regularly on one of the two most important standing committees in either house (for example, Finance).

Examination of relevant data (see Table 15) indicates that 20 percent (nine) of all senators in 1966 were directors or director-stockholders in the top group mentioned above. If we add to this participation in any one of the *sociedades anónimas*, insurance companies, or banks existing at the end of 1966, the number increases to 27 percent (twelve). The respective percentages and numbers for the Chamber are 0.7 percent (one) and 5 percent (seven). At least two secretaries of Senate standing committees are also directors of director-stockholders in several companies—one in the same company as a senator. In one case, two senators of ideologically opposed political parties are directors on the same company.[62]

CONCLUSION

The Senate does play an important role in the policy-making process of the Chilean political system. The Senate also exercises considerable control over budgetary matters, despite a constitutional provision that gives the president exclusive jurisdiction in this area. The notion that presidential urgency powers give the executive an important advan-

---

[62] For possible implications of these ties, see Ricardo Lagos Escobar, *La concentración del poder económico: Su teoría, realidad chilena*, pp. 168–177.

TABLE 15: 1966 Senators and Deputies Who Are Directors or Director-Stockholders in Top Group or Total Group by Party

| | Top Group | | | | | | | Total Group[a] | | | | | | |
	PC	PS	PDC	PR	PN	Total	%	PC	PS	PDC	PR	PN	Total	%
Senators	—	1	—	3	5	9	20	—	2	—	5	5	12	27
Deputies	—	—	—	—	1	1	0.7	—	—	4	2	1	7	5
Total	—	1	—	3	6	10	6	—	2	4	7	6	19	10

SOURCE: Compiled from raw data provided by the Superintendencia de Compañías de Seguros, Sociedades Anónimas y Bolsas de Comercio and by the Superintendencia del Bancos.

[a] Not including congressmen who were only stockholders or formerly associated as above during their terms. Independent Senators are grouped with party that supports them in elections.

tage over the Senate in the initiation and evaluation of policy is not supported by my exploratory research. Not only is the Senate able to delay or reject a presidential measure labeled urgent, but it also has used this presidential power to its own advantage by initiating and attaching numerous new bills to the coattails of an urgency measure. The president is frequently forced to accept these riders if he desires the passage of his own legislation.

The Senate exercises considerable control over the administrative bureaucracy as well. The Senate's rather extraordinary power vis-à-vis other political institutions rest in part upon the prestige ascribed to that institution. This prestige is in turn a function of institutional performance; such factors as long experience, informal behavioral norms that encourage expertise, and relatively elaborate supporting services permit senators to perform their tasks in a manner that cumulatively makes the Senate a power within the Chilean political system.

2. Autonomy of Senate Committees

ONE OF THE MOST PROVOCATIVE statements in Jewell and Patterson's recent textbook on the American legislative process is that there is an inherent contradiction between party and committee leadership! "Where committees are strong and independent, party leadership is weak. Where party leadership is strong, the committees are either weak or simply agents of the party leaders." As an example, the authors argue that congressional committees in the United States are strong, proud, and independent, whereas the leadership of political parties is comparatively weak.[1] This independence is based in part on

NOTE: Portions of this chapter originally appeared in the *Journal of Latin American Studies* 2, pt. 1 (1970) and are used here in revised form with the permission of the publisher.

[1] Malcolm E. Jewell and Samuel C. Patterson, *The Legislative Process in the United States*, pp. 203, 204.

the fact that chairmen of committees are selected by seniority and traditionally have not been removed by party leaders. Party lines are often crossed in the voting within committee, and chairmen have considerable say over whether a bill will be reported out or not.

In contrast, the political parties in the British House of Commons are strong and relatively unified, the committees comparatively weak. Herman Finer notes that the committees lack continuous jurisdiction, have a fluctuating membership, and do not possess the power of life and death over bills.[2]

A survey of the existing literature on the relationship between Chilean Senate committee independence and party leadership does not yield similarly clear-cut conclusions. On the one hand, a case may be made that Senate committees have considerable independence from political party leaders. Carlos Andrade Geywitz notes that it is in committees where real study and compromise takes place.[3] As in the U.S. Congress, members frequently stay on the same committee for years and acquire a specialized knowledge on the matters of the committees. Federico Gil points out that the bulk of legislation originates in committee and reports are rarely modified before passage on the floor.[4] On the other hand, committees may be simply intervening variables, with the national executive committees of the various political parties acting as the independent variable. Some writers have suggested that the national executive committees outside and floor leaders inside the Senate exercise some influence over recruitment of members and presidents to committees at the beginning of and during the legislative period.[5] Furthermore, there is no seniority system or tradition that prohibits censure of committee presidents as in the U.S. Congress.

Similarly, evidence for the strength of political party leadership, which has an important bearing on determining just how much autonomy Senate committees actually have, indicates that it is probably stronger than in U.S. parties, but perhaps less than in English parties.

---

[2] Herman Finer, *Governments of Greater European Powers*, p. 116.

[3] Carlos Andrade Geywitz, *Elementos de derecho constitucional chileno*, p. 444.

[4] Federico G. Gil, *The Political System of Chile*, p. 111.

[5] See, for example, Ingrid Ahumada Muñoz, *Las comisiones parlamentarias en Chile y otros países*, p. 62.

Scholars normally describe Chilean political parties as highly central-ized and more disciplined than U.S. parties.[6] Although no roll-call studies have been completed in Chile, these scholars probably would expect to find the level of discipline comparable with that of British political parties. Candidates for political office seem to depend more on the national party leadership for their nomination, placement on the ballot, and election. Party orders are issued as to how Senate mem-bers should vote on important issues, and senators have been expelled from party membership for failure to follow the party line, particu-larly among parties of the Left (the senator does not lose his seat, how-ever).[7]

But, even if Chilean political parties are highly centralized, the level of discipline appears to vary markedly from party to party. For example, Federico Gil has characterized the Radical party, one of the two largest parties in the Senate, as "individualistic" and "absent of any rigid discipline."[8] The Christian-Democrat party, the largest in the Senate, is split internally into at least three clear factions. There is some evidence that one way the party holds itself together is by tolerat-ing divergent voting patterns on some bills—even when party orders (instructions on how to vote in committee and on the floor) have been issued. In the National party, Senator Francisco Bulnes seems to have more influence on the national executive committee's decisions than vice-versa.[9] Furthermore, Chilean senators are noted for their highly individualistic nature, which helps explain the deep factional splits among Socialist senators and the fact that several senators are seated as independents. Also, as noted earlier, most senators are elected repeatedly by the same district, as in the U.S. Senate. Voting for constituency interests is frequently regarded as a legitimate reason to vote contrary to party orders, except perhaps for the Communist party.

Senate committees have an autonomous base of influence, inde-pendent of national party leadership, the sources of which include

---

[6] Gilberto Moreno G., *Los comités parlamentarios*, pp. 70–81.
[7] *Ibid.*, pp. 37–51.
[8] Gil, *Political System of Chile*, p. 265.
[9] J. Rogers Sotomayer, "Democracia 'representativa' y representación 'dele-gada,' " *Política, Economía, Cultura*, no. 259 (December 15, 1967), pp. 9–10.

(1) a limited and not always effective party discipline and (2) the ambience of the committee itself, in which, on some key and most ordinary issues, accepted norms promote cooperation and compromise over partisanship and so affect the decision-making process.

More specifically, Senate expectations limit the use of orders on how to vote by national party leadership to issues of major magnitude that clearly divide the various political parties ideologically. Even then, although overall discipline appears to be stronger than for U.S. parties, it varies by party, by issue, and even by specific amendments to a key bill. Furthermore, even when national party orders are followed, senators exercise a strong influence on the position actually taken by the party because of their key committee positions or because they may head the national party or belong to the executive committee that issues party orders.

On the many issues where there are no party orders, decisions are reached in Senate committees. The committee environment and internal norms of expertise, specialization, and consideration of the national interest soften and frequently offset partisanship. For example, the smallness of the committee (five members) and the fact that sessions are closed and off the record encourage a friendly impersonal style that is conducive to a candid exchange of views and interparty agreements. This is reinforced by committee norms and a nonpartisan staff.

Additional evidence suggests that Senate committees are an important center for decision-making. Executive officials regularly appear before committees to defend bills or make compromise agreements, and most committee reports not controlled by orders from the national parties' leadership are accepted on the Senate floor. Pending future research, we conclude that Senate committees exercise autonomous influence on many issues where there are no national party orders and in some cases even when there are.

POLITICAL PARTY DISCIPLINE

If Jewell and Patterson's statement that there is an inherent contradiction between party and committee leadership is correct, one means of determining how much autonomy Senate committees have is to find out how frequently national party orders are issued and how strong discipline is by party. Senators and staff interviews indicate that all political parties except the Communist party issue orders only on major issues that split the parties along clear ideological lines. Bills mentioned as examples were the Agrarian Reform Bill of 1966, which amended Article 10, Section 10, of the Constitution on property rights; the Copper Bill of 1966, which Chileanized the industry; and the Salary Readjustment Bill of 1968. Take these statements, for example: "There is strong party discipline on doctrinaire issues, but on all other bills a senator is free to vote as he chooses"; "The normal rule is that senators come to committees without instructions from their party."

The Senate has the power to perform certain judicial functions, such as interpreting the Constitution as it relates to particular bills; ruling on the interpretation of Senate Rules; and deciding cases of censure, such as ministers of state, senators, and mayors. When these matters are before the Senate Committee of Constitution, Legislation, Justice, and Rules or on the floor, senators do not expect to receive party orders.[10] This is also true when the body must decide whether or not to grant the president of the republic permission to travel abroad, or pass on diplomatic appointments.

The conflict of interest charge made in 1963 against Senator Bulnes provides a good example of this latitude. Bulnes owns a profitable Volvo import business as well as being a senator. Charges were made that Bulnes' private interests conflicted with his public career. When the issue came to a vote on the Senate floor, PDC Senator Eduardo Frei voted for censure, whereas Tomás Pablo of the same party did not.[11]

Except for the Communist party, Chilean senators are said to be

[10] This norm is not always observed. Some committee reports and floor debates turn into highly partisan debates, as happened with the Committee of Constitution, Legislation, Justice, and Rules report on Senator Carlos Altamirano in 1967. Altamirano had been jailed for personally slandering the president of the republic and the armed forces. The committee reported on whether he should lose his right to attend and vote in Senate sessions, and votes followed party lines. Furthermore, partisanship became so strong that the minority issued a separate report.

[11] Based on interview response and cross-check of votes on the floor in Senate debates.

characterized by a highly individualistic style in relation to their national party leadership. They appreciate the functions served by party discipline and support the use of orders on key issues. But, in exchange, senators expect freedom on all other matters. These expectations limit when party orders may be legitimately used and go a long way to explain the discretionary use of such orders.[12]

Interviews are particularly revealing in this regard. One might expect that a senator from the government party (PDC) who also had recently been its national president might favor broad use of party orders. Contrast this assumption with his interview remarks: "I think orders serve a useful purpose, but they should be used prudently, not habitually. If this is not the practice, it means the head of the party has replaced parliament." Said another: "Senators are mature men and can make up their own minds. . . . My view is that there should be orders only on key issues, and then only in the form of recommendations. Senators are elected by the people, not the party."

Occasionally, senators may even buck national party orders on key bills. For example, the National party caucus decided to vote against party orders on an important article of the 1968 Salary Readjustment Bill. One member of this group reflected his national role when he explained his vote: "In my view, a congressman has a responsibility to the interests of the country before his party. That's exactly how we voted on this bill." Probably the most influential staff member in the Senate explained just how much discipline senators are willing to accept: "You know, senators are not yes men. They oppose absolute party discipline, except for the Communist party. Once I made a proposal that a senator would lose his seat if he did not follow a party order. It really surprised me when the bulk of the senators opposed the idea. The reason simply is that they fear the national party leadership can be dictatorial on occasion, and they always want to have an escape route open."

Although the level of party discipline is probably somewhat higher overall than in U.S. parties, it should be emphasized that there is considerable variation by party. When senators were asked, "It is often

---

[12] Based on Peter M. Blau's discussion in *Exchange and Power in Social Life*, p. 215.

said that there is strong party discipline in Chile. Is this true?" 83 percent (thirty-five) of those responding (forty-two) said yes, once a party order is issued. Nine of these senators also made direct overall comparisons with the level of party discipline in the United States or Europe, such as this example: "There is more discipline than in the United States, less than in England, more than in France, and less than in Germany."

But clearly the level of discipline varies by party. Whenever possible, senators were also asked, "Does it vary by party?" *All* the senators responding to this question (eighteen asked) said yes, and fourteen of these volunteered unanimously that the Communist party was the most highly disciplined party (virtually 100%). A typical comment was that "no matter what the bill, the Communist party senators vote together. The rest of the parties are not the same." At the other end of the scale, several senators named the National party as least disciplined.

Attention was also drawn to short-term fluctuations. For example, the level of discipline for the Radical party following the 1964 presidential election defeat was said to be lower than in 1968. Similarly, the National party (formed in 1966 by the union of the Liberal and Conservative parties) seems to have augmented its level of internal discipline over the same period. Furthermore, senators who have had several years of congressional experience observed that the level of party discipline has increased for all parties over the last decade.[13]

So far, we have seen that normative expectations limit the use of national party orders and that, even when orders are issued, discipline varies by party. A corollary piece of evidence is that national party orders may pertain to the first stage of a crucial bill (whether or not to legislate) but frequently are *not* issued for the second stage, when the specific articles of the bill are examined. Furthermore, if orders are issued for both stages of a key bill, senators may ask for and

---

[13] The degree to which strict party-line voting does exist may be attributed in part to the national electoral law, which requires a large number of signatures before a man can run as a nonparty candidate, and in part to the need for campaign funds that national parties can provide. The latter factor has special impact for the PDC, the PS, and the PC.

normally are granted freedom to vote as they wish for constituency or conscience reasons. Even when a senator votes the party line against his personal wishes, he is free (except in the Communist party) to speak out publicly against the party position, and this may be effective in undermining it eventually.

Examination of recorded votes on the first stage of three important bills over the last two administrations (the 1962 Agrarian Reform Bill, the 1966 Agrarian Reform Bill, and the Chileanization Copper Bill) indicate strict party voting both in committees and on the floor. Unfortunately, specific article by article votes by each senator do not appear in committee reports or at the end of floor debates (although aggregate totals are available for the latter). It is therefore difficult to reach accurate conclusions on party discipline for the specific stages of these bills.

Nevertheless, interviews and personal observation during the passage of the 1968 Salary Readjustment Bill make some tentative statements possible. Interviews, newspaper quotations, and review of committee reports show that committee members entered the sessions on the general discussion of the bill (both times that the president submitted it to Congress) with party orders on how to vote. This fact explains why the Joint Finance and Government Committee reports were accepted on the floor. But, on specific review, several compromises across parties took place in committee, and senators were free to vote as they saw fit on several articles of the bill. We also noted that the secretary of the Senate records article roll calls on a printed form that is not subsequently placed in the public record. This suggests that unofficially these votes may be made available.

Personal interviews also show that senators from every party but the Communist party wrangle permission to vote contrary to national party orders at both the general and specific stages of a key bill. When senators were asked, "Are there circumstances when you believe it is not necessary for a member to vote with his party?" the great majority (77%) of those responding (twenty-two) said yes. The occasions most frequently mentioned were when party orders conflict with constituency interests or the senator's conscience.

A committee secretary described the cross-pressures a senator faces when his party orders a vote contrary to his constituency's interest: "A senator is in a real bind when his party asks him to vote against a project that is in the interest of his district. . . . The party might say, 'we have paid the cost of your last campaign.' At the same time, he is receiving telegrams from his district urging a vote the other way." A senator normally seeks to resolve this conflict by asking the party leadership for freedom to vote contrary to party orders.[14] One senator noted, with obvious pleasure: "On the Austral University Bill, I sought and received permission to vote for the project. I just couldn't vote against what was evidently good for my district. As it turned out, my vote was the one that passed it." According to a Christian-Democrat senator, even a Communist congressman bucked a party order on the same grounds some years ago.

Matters of conscience are another cause for objecting to a party order. As a rule, this involves important bills that exhort a senator to elevate national interest above partisanship. For example, one senator who represented his party on the Finance Committee spoke in favor of supporting the party line—up to a point. "I favor supporting the party, but I'm not going to vote against my conscience. The way I resolve the matter is to say, 'Look, party, let me pair or replace me on committee.' That way we both save face."

If a party has the required majority to pass a bill either individually or jointly in bloc with other parties, several alternative means are available that enable both the national party leadership and the senator to save face once the bill comes to the floor. The most subtle means is for the senator simply to walk out or not appear before a vote is taken. Here the party bears little or no cost, since it has a safe majority, and the senator satisfies his conscience by not giving further support. A middle range of alternative actions are for the senator to pair or abstain. Here the action symbolizes a more overt parting with the party line, but it is still prudent enough to avoid any lasting damage. Finally, the senator may cast his vote in opposition to the party line. This course of action involves an increment in cost both to the party

---

[14] For a discussion of conflicting role orientations in four American state legislatures, see John C. Wahlke *et al.*, *The Legislative System: Explorations in Legislative Behavior*, chs. 11–15.

and to the senator in question. Although loss of his vote does not affect the outcome of this particular bill, it does tend to aggravate intraparty differences that may exist. Also, the vote offers the press an opportunity to add fuel to the fire by publicizing splits in the party ranks. The party, in return, may be forced to take some measure of disciplinary action, if for nothing more than to quiet the public press.

When a party or bloc has a majority vote assured, it normally allows the senator to opt for one of the alternatives outlined above. If a majority is lacking, however, permission to break with the party is not likely. Now the senator has two main options. The first and most frequently used is to vote with the party or bloc, but to disagree publicly with its stand. Here a clear break is made with the party leadership, and this may create sufficient internal dissension to split the party sharply into factions (as may be seen for the Radical, Christian-Democrat, and Socialist parties for the 1964–1968 period). Although this action is probably not sufficient grounds for expulsion from the party, a senator may be pressured to tone down his attacks or to refrain from washing the party linen in public. One senator, reflecting on the past, said: "I was a rebel in the party. When I felt an order was not in the interests of the country, I said so. But I suffered a lot of damage (*daños*) as a result."

Although tolerance of public stands against the leadership may produce dysfunctional conflict, it also provides a necessary outlet for the release of short-term hostility, which is functional to the preservation of the group.[15] One perceptive senator concluded: "You will often see senators voting with their party but stating on the floor that they personally oppose the bill. I'm for this. It allows the senator to maintain his individuality. This dissipates hostility and helps to sustain a friendly atmosphere."

The second and most severe affront a senator can make is to vote against his party or bloc. In this case, maximum costs are likely to be incurred. The party loses a vote on a key bill, and the senator is subject to censure and even purge from the party. The fact that such votes do

---

[15] See Lewis A. Coser's discussion of communal conflict and noncommunal conflict in *The Functions of Social Conflict*, pp. 81–82.

occur is testimony not only to the individualistic style of many senators, but also to the effective level of party discipline.

An example was observed during the passage of the 1968 Salary Readjustment Bill. While committee discussions were in progress, an interest group called the Committee for the Defense of the Taxpayer pressured for maintaining taxes at the existing level, at the same time urging increases in other benefits. One PN senator said at the time: "They don't want any change in taxes, but they want more benefits. There just isn't any head or tail to that position." The outcome was that the PN senators opposed the national party orders, and voted accordingly on the floor.

Extensive research is required to unlock all the doors to explaining how such votes are possible, particularly among the center-right parties. One thing is clear—threats of censure or purge in the National, Radical, and Christian-Democrat parties seem to have less impact than had been expected, and certainly less than is true for the Communist party. One probable explanation is that a greater number of the senators in these parties have adequate independent means to finance campaign expenditures. Second, some parties simply cannot afford to lose a popular candidate who may have sufficient drawing power to carry other candidates on the party list into office with him.[16] Finally, one may ask, where do purged senators go? *They do not lose their seats.* It appears that many simply join another party. At least seven (16%) of the present Senate membership have at one time or another in their career been a member of at least one other party.

Herein is a partial clue to why Senate committees may have some autonomy from national political parties. Several senators have been members of more than one party over the years. This weakens partisan cues and enables senators to identify more easily with the broad national interest. In addition, elites have traditionally been accustomed

---

[16] Chilean congressmen are elected on a party-list basis for each district. All votes for a party are divided by a quotient formula that determines how many party candidates are elected. Hence, a good vote-getter on the list can pull other senators from the same party in on his coattails. See, for example, "Methods of Electing National Executives and National Legislatures in South America," Institute for the Comparative Study of Political Systems, *Special Memorandum* no. 21, pp. 9–11.

to working in cross-party blocs that inculcate habits of cooperation and compromise. These factors predispose senators to temper norms of partisanship (or at least to set acceptable bounds for it).

Senate Committee Membership and Party Policy

Thus far we have examined the degree to which party discipline effectively exists by party, by bill, and by sections of a bill. We have noted that the level of discipline varies, increasing in degree as one moves from Left to Right in the political spectrum. Still, discipline is probably higher than for U.S. parties. On many key bills, national party orders are obeyed. On these occasions, one might surmise that Senate committee votes become a mere formality, reflecting party orders taken beforehand. During the Woodrow Wilson administration, committees in the U.S. House of Representatives functioned in this manner. Political party caucuses often agreed on the details of a bill before it was introduced or issued instructions on how to vote. As a result, committees had much less independence from political party leadership than they have today.[17]

This is certainly one possibility. We noted earlier that firsthand personal observation of the passage of the 1968 Salary Readjustment Bill indicated that members of the Finance and Government committees meeting jointly received orders on how to vote for the general discussion of the bill before committee sessions began. When this occurs, acceptance of the committee report on the floor indicates the strength of party leadership rather than committee autonomy or deference to the committee's expertise. Interviews also show that on some occasions a committee may begin sessions with no party orders and report out a bill, only to have it rejected on the floor because a majority of the parties' leadership ordered a vote against it after committee sessions but before floor action. This happened, for example, during the passage of the 1966 Chileanization Copper Bill. Here again, party leadership rather than committee independence is suggested.

But for some parties, at least, the executive committee of each of

[17] Wilder H. Haines, "The Congressional Caucus of Today," *American Political Science Review* 9 (1915): 696–706.

the various parties, which determines policy stands, may also act as an intervening variable, with the Senate committee (by virtue of a senator's overlapping membership) being the independent variable. Congressmen, particularly senators, are represented on national party executive committees either as members or as president of the party and are therefore in a position to influence party policy itself. Simultaneously, they are frequently members of top Senate committees as well. Committees are one center where specific knowledge of a bill's contents is gained, and this may give a senator sufficient leverage to sway party policy.

Let's turn now to some specific data. In 1968, every president of the national parties except the National party were senators. When the membership of the policy-making executive committees (or central committees) are examined we see that at least two and sometimes three senators are represented (see Tables 16 and 17). On political matters, such as the party's stand on a bill, part of the membership of the executive committee (or central committee) breaks into smaller units called political committees. Interviews suggest that these smaller committees effectively determine the direction of party discipline. If this is true, it appears to augment the potential influence of senators on national party decision-making. For the three parties where data were available (PR, PS, and PC), senators account for a minimum of 27 percent (PC) to a maximum of 43 percent (PR) of the membership versus a minimum of 5 percent and a maximum of 16 percent for the national committee membership.

Examination of the membership of the top five committees reveals considerable overlap with that of the respective leadership of the various national parties (Table 18). Interviews indicate that senators use knowledge gained from committee deliberations to sway national party policy, and this influence is decisive in the National and Radical parties, important in the Christian-Democrat party, and relatively less important in the Socialist and Communist parties. Senators were asked, "Does it ever happen that senators, knowledgeable on certain bills studied in a committee, influence the position their political party takes on that bill?" Of the thirty-three who answered this question, a majority (52%, or seventeen) felt that senators were able to sway party

TABLE 16: Senators Represented on National Executive Committee, 1968

Party	President of Party and a Senator	Executive Committee Total No.	No. Senators	%	Names
PN	—	27	2	7	Bulnes, Ibáñez
PR	Miranda	26	2	8	Miranda, Ahumada
PDC	Fuentealba	19	3	16	Reyes, Fuentealba, Palma
PS	Rodríguez	15	2	14	Rodríguez, Altamirano
PC	Corvalán	55	3		Corvalán, Teitelboim, Campusano

SOURCE: Compiled from data supplied by each party headquarters.

TABLE 17: Senators Represented on National Political Committee, 1968

Party	Political Committee Total No.	No. Senators	%	Names
PN	—	—	—	—
PR	7	3	43	Bossay, Baltra, Aguirre
PDC	—	—	—	—
PS	7	2	29	Rodríguez, Altamirano
PC	11	3	27	Corvalán, Teitelboim, Campusano

SOURCE: Compiled from data supplied by each party headquarters.

policy a lot or a great deal, 46 percent (fifteen) some or not too much, and 3 percent (one) not at all. Take these sample comments: "Committee members orient party votes" (PDC); "On specialized matters, we can have a lot of influence" (PR); "At times there are conflicts with the party leadership, and we have asked them to change their stand" (PN). Socialist senators are listened to, but other members

TABLE 18: Senators on Party Policy Organs Who Are Also Members of Top Senate Committees

Finance	Constitution, Legislation, Justice, and Rules	Labor and Social Legislation	National Defense	Foreign Relations
Altamirano (PS)	Ahumada (PR)	Rodríguez (PS)	Aguirre (PR)	Fuentealba (PDC)
Bossay (PR)			Teitelboim (PC)	Teitelboim (PC)
Palma (PDC)				

SOURCE: Compiled from data supplied by each party headquarters and Senate committee membership file, 1965–1968.

of the leadership tend to balance their influence. Said one Socialist senator: "Senators in the center-right parties have more influence. For us, the party leadership as a whole has the final say." Similarly, Communist senators express their views but do not appear to hold any more weight than other members of the party leadership. One staff member summarized his perceptions of the impact of senators' knowledge and expertise on policy by party as shown in Table 19.

Interviews also show that senators' influence varies by type of bill, their spokesman on the national party executive committee, and whether senators are in total agreement or split among themselves. A senator explained: "Each chamber of Congress has a representative on the executive committee. Senators' impact on the final decision varies by law and the knowledge they have of it." Another, obviously irritated by recent press reports that Christian-Democrat senators were "yes men," burst out: "Those who talk of yes men are only trying to lower the prestige of Congress. We have representatives on the executive committee, and they speak with authority on bills. It just is that there are others in the party who also have specific knowledge, and this checks their influence somewhat."

When a bill affects a senator's district, he can speak with greater skill and assurance, and this sways the party. If the majority of an executive committee are inclined to vote one way and all the senators of that party speak in unison for the opposite position, the party is likely to opt for the senators. On the other hand, if senators are split among themselves, it tends to dissipate their impact on party policy.

A staff member noted that senators also influence party policy indirectly by advising the leadership what they think the opposition senators will accept. "The Christian-Democrats have a triparty arrangement where representatives from Congress, the administration, and the party all work together on a bill. The leaders of nearly all the parties are in the Senate, so Christian-Democrat senators are in a good position to tell the group how X felt in the committee meeting about this or that, and to urge compromise or changes."

COMMITTEE AUTONOMY

Internal Environment

A committee system will have a certain degree of autonomy from national party leadership if it serves as an arena for cross-party cooperation and compromise. One way to determine whether a committee system performs this function is to tap senator and staff perceptions on the level of partisanship in committees versus on the Senate floor. Therefore, we asked both groups, "When you study a bill in committee is there a lot of partisanship as on the floor?" All but one senator answered this question. The overwhelming majority of the senators (89%, or thirty-eight) considered the level of partisanship substantially less in committees than on the floor. Similarly, 91 percent of the staff members interviewed agreed.

A classic illustration of the capacity of the committee environment to socialize and depoliticize ideologically opposed senators was this senator's comment: "There is still partisanship, but a lower degree of it. It's easier to overcome in committees. . . . One thing I've observed with some experience here is that the longer you stay, the more you tend to identify with a solution. The new senator arrives with strong partisan feelings; he isn't attached to the committee work. But after a few years, he becomes less partisan, more mature; he begins to reason, and the committee becomes a meeting of friends." The end product of this process is the ability of opposing senators to work to-

TABLE 19: Discipline and Influence of Senators by Party

Party	Degree of Discipline	Influence of Senators on Party Policy
PC	Absolute	One factor
PS	Strong	Less important
PDC	More than PR but similar	Important
PR	Tends to be individualistic	Decisive
PN	Little	Absolute

gether when common goals are involved. This is revealed by one Communist senator's comments regarding two ideologically opposed National senators: "There is often serious analysis in committees . . . Jaramillo has voted for the interests of the workers several times in the Labor and Social Legislation Committee, and Bulnes I know studied hard on the 1966 Copper Bill."

Several elements linked together help encourage cross-party communication and compromise in committees. The membership is small, five senators and two staff members. Sessions are closed and off the record. If discussions are taped, this is solely to aid the secretary in writing the committee report, and the tapes are subsequently destroyed. There is no public gallery or press recording every comment. As a result, the dialogue is free and open, more like a club get-together than a formal committee meeting. Said one staff member: "There is a lot less partisanship in committees. One reason is that the sessions are private. If senators know what they are saying will not go out of the room, they work a lot better together." Personal exchanges are on a first name basis characterized by *tutuyas* (familiar *tu* versus formal use of *usted*). This climate is reinforced by the presence of a nonpartisan staff. One senator gave tribute to this function: "The staff and special experts cited to appear center the theme of the discussion, and this obliges a more thorough study." Another senator concluded his analogy between committee sessions and floor debates with this comment: "The floor debates serve a public relations function; the committee is the office of work."

Serious study in committees also serves one other important function. It enables senators to build a reputation for expertise in a certain subject matter, which in turn serves as a base of power, not only in committee but in the national party policy organs. Take these interview statements, for example: "The real Senate work is done here in committees. This is where you get to know each other, and prove your ability"; "In committees, you see the real man—this is where you talk about the interests of Chile, and less about party."

An interesting practice of giving votes to other members is one illustration of the level of comradeship and trust across parties in committee. For various reasons, many senators are members of several committees simultaneously. When two of these committees session at the same hour, a senator may appear to provide a quorum, give his proxy to another member, and leave to work in the other committee. When an issue comes up for a vote, the senator who holds two will cast the one held in trust the same way he knows the other senator would—even if it opposes his own vote. What enables this system to work is the recognition that maybe tomorrow or next week the trustee will want the opposition senator to reciprocate; this principle is extended as well to the pair system on the floor.[18]

This is not to suggest that norms of partisanship are totally displaced in Senate committees. One Radical senator observed: "There is certainly less partisanship, but never zero. You might say there is at least 20 percent all the time." Interviews and observation indicate that the level of partisanship in committees varies by type of bill, by stage of the bill (general versus specific discussion), by party, by committee, and by time period.

We saw earlier that party orders on some key bills may precede the general discussion in committee. On these occasions, partisanship is accentuated. But even then it is displaced by other norms during article-by-article review. For example, a Christian-Democrat senator noted that even though Radical Senator Luis Bossay had orders on

18 For a discussion of how personal identification with the system (i.e., giving each participant a stake in ensuring its survival) provides for reduction in the intensity of partisan considerations and displacement by system attachment and support, see Ralf Dahrendorf, *Class and Class Conflict in Industrial Society*, p. 216.

how to vote at the first stage of the 1968 Salary Readjustment Bill, he cooperated with the Christian-Democrat party later to eliminate several amendments. A staff member confessed: "A lot of amendments are cut out in committees. Many are submitted to meet district or pressure group demands. But, imagine, the *same* senator will take them out in committee."

Generally, committee norms of expertise and specialized study seem to predominate over partisan criteria when the content of the bill is highly technical. One staff member said: "There are two general kinds of bills, technical and partisan. When a committee goes over the former type, it works alone, free from political pressure." On the latter, the displacement process is reversed, and this is accentuated by the fact that parties of the Left tend to instruct their senators on how to vote more frequently than does the Right.

Very exploratory research also suggests that the level of partisanship may vary from committee to committee much as in the U.S. Congress (e.g., compare House Appropriations Committee to Ways and Means and to Education and Labor).[19] For example, the responsibility of interpreting the Constitution as well as the highly technical nature of most bills considered by the Constitution, Legislation, Justice, and Rules Committee cause members to emphasize norms of expertise and specialization rather than partisanship. On the other hand, many of the bills the Labor and Social Legislation Committee considers involve issues on which the political parties disagree ideologically (e.g., social security benefits, right to strike). As a result, interest-group activity is more evident, and discussions more often tend to be high pitched speeches instead of calm, careful reviews. Also, such circumstantial variables as a coming election period or animosities left as the result of a previous campaign (e.g., 1965) may raise or lower the influence of one set of norms over the other. Still, as a whole, a quiet, private, and informal committee environment reduces partisan conflict—or at least provides an arena where compromises can be pounded out.

---

[19] See Nicholas A. Masters' comments in "Committee Assignments in the House of Representatives," in *New Perspectives on the House of Representatives*, ed. Robert L. Peabody and Nelson W. Polsby, pp. 53–56.

Executive Branch Contact

Another means of determining whether a committee system acts as an independent center for decision-making is to observe whether committees have frequent contact with the executive branch and, if so, to discern whether these contacts are only symbolic in nature or exhibit some measure of the committees' independent power.

Senate interviews and personal observation confirm that contacts are regular and continuous. Senators and staff were asked, "As a general rule, does a standing committee have much contact with the executive branch during your committee work?" *Every* senator and staff member answering this question (thirty-six and fifteen, respectively) said yes.

Once the president of the Republic presents a bill for Senate consideration and it is assigned to the pertinent committee, hearings are called. Experts, interest groups, and ministers and their staffs are cited to give testimony. One of the chief tasks of the committee is to determine what the facts actually are before it can act. This is not an easy task.

Consider the question of whether a bill has adequate financing. One of the Finance Committee's responsibilities is to determine whether there are adequate budget funds for proposed legislation. Centering on this task, the committee begins with the reality that government figures may not be totally objective or reliable. Said one senator: "It has been traditional every year for the administration to say, 'We don't have funds for this project or that.' But they are always holding out on us, or channeling funds to one of their pet projects." This task is further complicated because budget resources are dependent on international copper prices. Surpluses and deficits can come and go almost overnight. Furthermore, anticipating future rates of inflation is virtually impossible. Finally, the committee must resolve for themselves what "financed" means. As mentioned earlier, "being financed" often means that today's expenditures are covered by earmarking funds in the coming year's budget. The committee attempts to fulfill its responsibility by collecting and cross-checking the available evidence. Therefore, a finance minister will be asked to appear to explain the discrepancy between his figures and a report prepared by OIS or a professor's expert testimony.

It is clear that the outcome of this process usually means modification or amendments to executive legislation (see chapter 1). Whether these changes represent improvements depends on one's vantage point. In any event, ministers regularly appear before committees to defend administration bills, and they try to discourage excessive amendments. According to one staff member, some executive officials are more effective in achieving this objective than others: "In my twelve or thirteen years of experience, I have seen that some executive officials greatly influence committee decisions. For example, the subsecretary of Social Legislation is independent politically, and so he is listened to carefully." Personal interviews in the executive branch indicate that a considerable amount of time is devoted by ministers and their staffs to preparing for committee hearings. If a minister is thoroughly familiar with his proposal and has the answers to committee questions, his credibility increases, as does his influence on committee decisions. Another technique occasionally used is for a minister to speak privately with each of the committee members before hearings begin. Apparently, Education Minister Maximó Pacheco employed this method before the 1968 Education Reform Bill was taken up formally. But, if a minister continually appears flustered, uncertain, or conflicting in his testimony, leaks will appear in the public press, and the president himself may have to begin making phone calls to salvage the bill.

Committee Reports on the Senate Floor

Committees' influence may also be measured by examining the success of their reports on the Senate floor. As noted earlier, this is not always true. When committee member votes have been predirected by national party orders, success of reports on the floor in effect reflects the strength of national party leadership and the intervening relationship of committees. But Senate committee members make decisions on several key and most intermediate and lower-range issues independent of party orders. In these instances, success of reports on the floor reflects the influence of Senate committees or, at the very least, of committee members as their respective parties' specialists.

Several scholars have stated that Senate committee reports are accepted approximately 90 per cent of the time on the floor,[20] and this figure was repeated in Senate and staff interviews. We were unable, however, to locate any empirical studies that show how this figure was arrived at, or that broke out figures for reports where votes were predirected by the national parties and for those that were not. Therefore we suggest they be used with caution. The interview and limited-bill data we have are quite exploratory and scattered, and require follow-up research. With these limitations in mind, we tentatively conclude that: (1) committee reports (both predirected votes by national parties and not) are normally accepted on the floor; (2) rejection of committee reports is caused by national party orders and the fact that some committees may not represent all the parties in the Senate.

Donald Matthews found that, in the U.S. Senate, when 80 percent or more of the members of a committee supported motions, they passed on the floor.[21] Interviews show a similar phenomenon in the Chilean Senate. A frequent remark was, "If 100 per cent of the committee favor a bill, there is little discussion on the floor." When committee unity is lower in the U.S. Senate, reports still frequently pass because congressmen defer to committee members as specialists and because these specialists are also leaders in their party.[22] When there are no national party orders, Chilean senators appear to accept committee reports for the same reasons. One senator noted, "Generally, committee reports are accepted on the floor because the study is more technical there." Another from an opposing party agreed: "Many articles are never discussed on the floor. We just accept the committee's view."

Why are committee reports rejected? There appear to be two prime causes. First, national party leaders may order a vote to reject the com-

20 See, for example, Jorge A. Tapia Valdés, *La técnica legislativa*, p. 30; Gil, *Political System of Chile*, pp. 115–122.

21 Donald R. Matthews, *U.S. Senators and Their World*, p. 169.

22 *Ibid*. Also see Richard F. Fenno, Jr., *The Power of the Purse: Appropriations Politics in Congress*, ch. 11. Fenno's perceptive comments on the overlap of Senate party leadership and membership on top committees is quite similar to the overlap of Chilean senators and national party policy organs discussed earlier.

mittee report *after* it has been released, or they may change their own position taken *prior* to the committee report after the committee report is released. An example of the former occurred in 1966 when the Radical party's executive committee issued orders to accept the Chileanization Copper Bill after the Finance Committee (including the Radical member) had voted to reject it. As to the latter, the National party reversed its position prior to the Joint Finance and Government Committee's report and after its release on the 1968 Salary Readjustment Bill. Richard Fenno has demonstrated that the regular acceptance of U.S. House Appropriations Committee reports on the floor is linked in part to the absence of a centralized, tightly disciplined congressional party that makes demands on committee and House members.[23] The complete reverse is not the case in Chile. But national parties are relatively more centralized and do make a correspondingly larger number of demands on Senate committees and members on the floor. This accounts for a large number of the reports that fail on the Senate floor.

The second cause for rejecting a committee report is that the membership of the committee may not represent all the major political parties in the Senate. Take the Foreign Relations and Government committees, for example. Senator Sergio Sepúlveda filled the National party seat and became president of the Foreign Relations Committee in 1965 as a result of the party bloc arrangement discussed earlier. In 1966, Sepúlveda broke with the National party and became an independent. Surprisingly, the National party did not remove him from the Foreign Relations Committee and fill the seat with a regular party member. As a result, the National party does not now have a member on the committee. Furthermore, Senators Baltazar Castro (VNP) and Volodia Teitelboim (PC) occupy the two seats for the leftist bloc of parties.[24] As a result, no Socialist senator sits on the committee either. Hence, committee reports can potentially be overturned on the floor because two of the five major parties are not represented there. This occurred in 1968 when the committee report calling for the acceptance of President Frei's diplomatic appointment to Peru was rejected on the

[23] Fenno, *The Power of the Purse*, p. 252.
[24] The system for distributing committee seats by party or party bloc is discussed in chapter 4.

floor. The same could happen to the Government Committee, where the Communist party is not represented either.

SUMMARY AND CONCLUSIONS

Senate committees may enjoy considerable autonomy in relation to national party leadership, but the level is probably less than is characteristic of U.S. congressional committees. Normative expectations and a highly individualistic Senate style limit the use of party orders to a few key bills. When issued, orders frequently do not apply to both the general and specific stages of bills, and, even when they do, senators are able to wrangle a series of exceptions.

The level of discipline also seems to vary by party, by bill, and even article by article within a bill. There is some evidence to indicate that committee decisions on some important bills are mere formalities, reflecting party orders taken beforehand. But on some key bills senators use committee deliberations to sway national party policy, and this influence is decisive or important for the majority of Chilean political parties. Also, several senators have been members of more than one political party during their career. This fact, combined with a tradition of cross-party bloc accommodation in order to pass legislation, may predispose senators to temper partisanship.

Several other indicators suggest that Senate committees have an important independent influence on legislative decisions. First of all, the committee environment (e.g., small size, closed sessions) helps to reduce partisanship, and thereby makes committees an arena for interparty accommodation and agreement. Senate committees also have frequent contact through hearings with the executive branch, which often leads to modification and amendment of key legislation. Finally, most committee reports that are *not* the subject of national party orders pass on the Senate floor in deference to committee expertise or greater knowledge.

3. Ranking of Senate Committees

ESTABLISHING THAT STANDING COMMITTEES exercise considerable power and autonomy in the Chilean Senate is only a first step toward defining and describing the internal distribution of influence of this body. If recent research on U.S. congressional committees is any indication, we can expect some Chilean Senate committees to enjoy more influence than others.[1] Therefore, the next logical step is to determine whether there is such a ranking, which, in turn, should tell us a good deal more about the distribution of power in the Senate

[1] Several studies have been conducted that show a rank order of committees in both houses of the U.S. Congress. See for example, Donald R. Matthews, *U.S. Senators and Their World*, pp. 148–158; and Warren E. Miller and Donald E. Stokes, *Representation in Congress*, cited in John F. Manley, "The House Committee on Ways and Means: 1947–1966" (Ph.D. dissertation, Syracuse University, 1967), pp. 42–43.

(e.g., who the potentially powerful senators are),[2] as well as explain other Senate behavior (e.g., intraparty fights over some committee seats).

A survey of Senate and staff interviews and five additional objective indicators identify the top five committees: the Finance Committee, the Constitution, Legislation, Justice, and Rules Committee, the Government Committee, the Labor and Social Legislation Committee, and the Foreign Relations Committee. The three least important are the Matters of Benefaction Committee, the Economy and Commerce Committee, and the Mining Committee. The remaining committees rank somewhere between these two groups. Senators rank committees according to the type of bills handled and the breadth of their impact, the work of a committee as measured by its sessions and reports, their own personal preferences, and temporal factors. Finally, rank order varies over time as work loads shift from one committee to another in response to the country's economic and political development.

INTERVIEW RANKING OF COMMITTEES

Senators and staff members were asked: "It is said that some standing committees are more important than others in the Senate. Is this so?" If the response was affirmative, they were also asked, "Which are the three most important and three least important ones in your opinion?" All forty-four senators responded affirmatively to the first part of the question, and there was an overwhelming consensus among senators that Finance is the top committee. Eighty-six percent (thirty-eight) ranked it first; the remaining first place votes (14%, or six) were distributed among four different committees. A smaller number of the senators made second and third place choices (86%, or thirty-eight, and 68%, or thirty, respectively). Even so, for our purposes the samples are large enough to construct an index. If three points are given to first place votes, two to second place, and one to third place,

[2] Richard F. Fenno, Jr., has stated that influential leaders in the U.S. House of Representatives must be sought among the most influential House committees. This may also be true in the Chilean Senate. See Richard F. Fenno, Jr., "The Internal Distribution of Influence: The House," in *The Congress and America's Future*, ed. David B. Truman, pp. 55.

Senate committees are ranked by senators as follows: (1) Finance, (2) Constitution, Legislation, Justice, and Rules, (3) Government, (4) Labor and Social Legislation, and (5) Foreign Relations (see Table 20).

One means of determining the reliability of the senators' perceptions (and responses) is to ask staff members the same question. Chilean Senate staff members are highly respected for their objectivity, expertise, and long career experience.[3] If their responses coincided with that of the senators, it would suggest that our committee ranking is relatively accurate.

Staff responses were virtually identical to those of the senators. Twenty of the twenty-one answering this question considered certain committees more important than others, and 85 percent (seventeen) ranked Finance first. Using the same point system as with senators' choices, we find that their ranking of the top four committees matches that for the senators (see Table 21).

Many senators and staff members had difficulty ranking the three least important committees, and four senators said that they considered the remaining committees of equal importance. Still, fifteen senators and six staff members did indicate an ordering, and there is considerable agreement as to which committees make up the list, despite some variation as to the exact rank. Individual responses indexed in Table 22 show that nine senators and four staff members agree that the Matters of Benefaction Committee is least important; both groups also mention Economy and Commerce, Mining, and Internal Police.

Interview Comments on Top Committees

Interview comments reveal why senators rank Finance, Constitution, Legislation, Justice, and Rules, Government, and Labor and Social Legislation as the top four committees. Finance is regarded as the queen of committees because of (1) formal prerogatives, (2) jurisdiction over nonfinancial aspects of important bills, which in turn is a product of informal custom and tradition, and (3) the experience, prestige, and publicity it affords its members.

[3] For example, committee staffs are not divided along partisan lines. They, as well as OIS, are available to serve all senators regardless of party.

TABLE 20: Index of Top Five Senate Committees (Senators)

Committee Rank	Votes			Total Points[a]
	First	Second	Third	
1. Finance	38	3	1	121
2. Constitution, Legislation, Justice, and Rules	2	13	9	41
3. Government	1	6	8	23
4. Labor and Social Legislation	2	6	3	21
5. Foreign Relations	—	6	5	17

[a] Total points are calculated by multiplying first place votes by three, second place by two, and third place by one.

TABLE 21: Index of Top Four Senate Committees (Staff)

Committee Rank	Votes			Total Points[a]
	First	Second	Third	
1. Finance	17	3	—	57
2. Constitution, Legislation, Justice, and Rules	9	26	—	35
3. Government	—	2	4	6
4. Labor and Social Legislation	—	—	3	3

[a] Total points are calculated by multiplying first place votes by three, second place by two, and third place by one.

Article 38 of the Senate Rules requires that *all* bills that signify appropriations not included in the annual budget or that call for new taxes must be reported on by Finance in addition to the relevant subject matter committee. This gatekeeper role of deciding whether or not important bills can be financed gives the committee and its members influence comparable to a cross between the U.S. Senate Finance and the House Appropriations committees. One senator's comment illus-

TABLE 22: Index of Three Least Important Senate Standing Committees (Senators and Staff)

Committee Rank[b]	Vote			Total Points[a]
	Least	Second to Least	Third to Least	
By senators				
1. Matters of Benefaction	9	2	—	31
2. Economy and Commerce	1	4	2	13
3. Internal Police	—	1	2	4
4. Mining	—	1	—	2
By staff				
1. Matters of Benefaction	4	—	—	12
2. Mining	—	4	—	8
3. Public Health	1	—	2	5
4. Economy and Commerce	—	—	2	2
5. Internal Police	—	1	—	2
By combined senators and staff				
1. Matters of Benefaction	13	2	—	43
2. Economy and Commerce	1	4	4	15
3. Mining	—	5	—	10
4. Internal Police	—	2	2	6

[a] Total points are calculated by multiplying least important by three, second to least by two, and third to least by one.

[b] Numbering from one to four runs from least important (1) to increasing degrees of importance.

trates this fact: "The Finance Committee is to a certain degree the arbitrator of other committees' decisions."

Theoretically, Finance should limit itself to determining whether a bill can be financed, leaving other aspects of the bill to subject matter committees. In fact, the practice is quite different. Over the years, customs and tradition have grown that allow Finance to extend its jurisdiction to include decisions as to the content of a bill and how the money provided for it will be spent. One senator notes, "The Finance Committee reviews not only the financing of a project, but the makeup of the bill itself." Said another, "The best ideas in the world don't come to pass without Finance." Finance also overshadows its sister committee, Economy and Commerce, which probably explains why senators rank the latter at the bottom of their list. One senator said, "Projects which in theory should go to Economy and Commerce are absorbed by Finance." In part, this practice is an outgrowth of the fact that Finance is a much older committee than Economy and Commerce. One senator who has the historical perspective that only a long congressional career can give said, "Economy and Commerce was created after Finance, and it just has never gained a foothold."

Deference to the Finance Committee's influence is evidenced by the fact that subject matter committees frequently meet jointly with her when important legislation is involved. In this way, they hope to avoid working over and reporting out a bill, only to have the Finance Committee reject or drastically modify its version as part of its financial review. This encroachment on other committees' jurisdiction has been the subject of frequent debate, and attempts have been made to limit the practice, but to little avail. One staff member tells how a new president of an unimportant committee tried to buck this practice: "Senator ———— once called a session to consider a bill without arranging a joint meeting with Finance. The members just simply didn't show up."

John Manley has found that the queen committee of the U.S. House (Ways and Means) attracts representatives because of the prestige and expertise membership provides. These benefits in turn predispose the members to be deferential to pre-existing workways.[4] A similar exchange relationship characterizes the Finance Committee. Take this typical senator's comment: "There is a certain tradition that most members want to work on Finance. The work is interesting, the committee is more decisive, and it gives prestige to the members." Because of its strategic role, press coverage is regularly kept on committee actions, and this may also aid members up for re-election or aspiring to the presidency.

Senators noted that a place on the Finance Committee "requires intensive work" in return. Interestingly, the internal style of the committee also resembles that of the U.S. House Ways and Means Committee. The specialized subject matter of the committee, along with the heavy responsibility of deciding which demands can and cannot be met, has

---

4 Manley, "House Committee on Ways and Means: 1947–1966," p. 47.

fostered a norm of restrained partisanship among its members. There is a lot of partisan voting because bills that come before the committee involve issues on which the political parties are ideologically divided. But members discuss the bill in a nonpartisan way. Senators describe the committee workways as "responsible," "thorough," and "studious."

The Constitution, Legislation, Justice, and Rules Committee is ranked second in importance because it has jurisdiction over legal and constitutional matters. For example, the committee decides whether a bill or its amendments have followed correct procedures or are constitutional, rules on internal Senate matters, and reports on motions for impeachment of the president, ministers, and other officials.[5] Senators view the committee as the "legal spirit and tradition of the Senate." One highly respected staff member stated: "Historically, it has acted in a manner not unlike the Anglo-Saxon tradition, flexibly interpreting the Constitution and the Senate Rules. I think this explains why we have a Constitution that has lasted since 1925."

Personal interviews and an examination of the career backgrounds of members from 1933 to 1968 indicate that only lawyers, professors of constitutional law, or experts in this field sit on the committee. Membership is comparatively stable,[6] and bills are reviewed calmly and seriously. Legal precedence and past committee decisions are always carefully reviewed before a report is issued. Although partisan interpretations occur periodically,[7] members are normally expected to devote their attention to the merits of the case in preference to party loyalties, and personal interviews and a reading of Senate debates show that senators object to party pressure to the contrary.

The Government, Labor and Social Legislation, and Foreign Rela-

[5] Normally, Constitution, Legislation, Justice, and Rules also considers constitutional reform bills. But floor leaders agreed in 1966 to set up a special committee to consider several pending reforms since the committee was already overburdened with other matters.

[6] See chapter 4 for data on the stability of membership on this committee for the period 1897 to 1965.

[7] An example was the report on whether Socialist Senator Carlos Altamirano could attend sessions and vote after a jail sentence as a result of his statements against the president and the military.

tions committees are ranked third, fourth, and fifth, respectively. The Government Committee is assigned all bills that affect the public administration (e.g., the 1968 Salary Readjustment Bill) and other aspects of the government. Senators find this committee important in part because it controls bills that affect their electoral fortunes. One senator remarked, "Government and Public Works grants rights or control funds that directly compromise the electoral interests of the senators."

The Labor and Social Legislation Committee handles such key legislation as that which sets guidelines for labor unions, work benefits, and social security legislation. Bills of this nature necessarily affect a large sector of the citizenry, and senators readily recognize the possible social and electoral implications. Interviews suggest that the committee is characterized by a greater degree of partisanship than the Finance or Constitution, Legislation, Justice, and Rules committees—not unlike the difference between the Education and Labor and Appropriations committees in the U.S. House.[8] Senators who champion the interests of labor seek to chair this committee, and one staff member notes, "I think pressure groups act more on Labor and Social Legislation than any other committee in the Senate." Interviews also indicate that this Committee has risen in prestige in recent years. This probably reflects the fact that, as Chile has developed economically and socially, marginal groups have been incorporated into the modern sector of society. This has led to the extension of social security benefits as well as to new labor legislation. Accordingly, the committee now has a heavier work load that affects a larger segment of the population than ever before.

The Foreign Relations Committee's fifth-place ranking puts it somewhere in the middle range of importance among the fourteen Senate committees. One of its bases of influence is the prerogative of review-

[8] Whereas members of the U.S. House Appropriations Committee stress a norm of minimal partisanship, members of the Education and Labor Committee are characterized by their partisanship. See for example, Richard F. Fenno, Jr., "The House Appropriations Committee as a Political System: The Problem of Integration," and Nicholas A. Masters, "Committee Assignments in the House of Representatives," both in *New Perspectives on the House of Representatives*, ed. Robert L. Peabody and Nelson W. Polsby, pp. 94 and 51, respectively.

ing diplomatic appointments of the president. On occasion, it will report out to reject an appointment, as we have seen. The committee may
also be called on by the president of the Republic for advice on a controversial foreign policy decision. Also significant is the fact that committee members frequently travel abroad. On these occasions, they are
formal representatives of their country, which places them in a highly
visible position that may involve Chile's international image. These
duties together give prestige to members. Still, the Foreign Relations
Committee does not stand at the top of the list of Senate preferences as
in the U.S. Senate, apparently because it has not developed the role of
foreign policy and executive review to the same degree as in the U.S.
Senate. One senator points out: "I prefer to sit on Foreign Relations
because I like to view the world as a whole, and our place in it. Unfortunately, we don't do as much of that as your Senator Fulbright does."
Another senator contends, "The President has the real leadership in
foreign affairs—not the Senate."

Least Important Committees

Senators and staff agree that Matters of Benefaction is the least important committee. Essentially, this committee handles only such personal patronage matters as the granting of pensions. The Senate attempts to keep pressure for benefits to a minimum by holding the
membership "secret," but it is doubtful that an interested party cannot
find out who he must see. The Economy and Commerce and Mining
committees are also ranked at the bottom. Senators claim that both
committees seldom meet. This is in part because the Finance Committee frequently assumes matters that should be assigned to these committees. Some senators felt that the Mining Committee should meet
more often either because Chile produces copper or because their district is tied more directly to this activity. Internal Police (chaired by the
president of the Senate) also ranks at the bottom of the list, as it handles only infrequent routine matters.

Method of Ranking and Variation over Time

Interviews indicated that four factors were taken into consideration
when ranking committees: (1) type of bills handled and the breadth

of their impact, (2) work of a committee as measured by reports, (3) temporal factors that might alter the ranking periodically, and (4) personal preferences. For example, one senator states: "Evidently some committees are more important. . . . It depends on how you divide it. Finance certainly is first if you mean the amount of work it does." Another contends that the Labor and Social Legislation Committee is the most important one because "the legislation it considers has a greater impact on the public." A third senator warned that his ranking was a temporal one: "Agriculture and Colonization is not a very important committee generally. But, when the agrarian reform came up, it became the center of attention for quite a while." Another said: "Mining hardly works at all. . . . But when the 1966 Copper Bill was discussed, it was important."

Donald R. Matthews finds that senators in the U.S. Senate do not all agree on committee preferences.[9] An examination of the preceding tables reveals that this is also the case in Chile. Finance stands at the top for most senators because of the training, experience, and national exposure membership affords. But others opt for the Constitution, Legislation, Justice, and Rules Committee because they are experts in this material and feel more comfortable there. Still other senators seek a seat on the Agriculture and Colonization Committee because their district is predominately rural or on the Public Works Committee in order to stimulate construction programs at home. One senator summarized the dispersion of preferences this way: "It all depends on the lens you look through."

OBJECTIVE CHECK OF INTERVIEW RESPONSE

Article 29 of the Senate Rules sets out an order of rank of Senate committees that does not match that described by senators and staff (see Table 23). For example, Senate Rules places the Labor and Social Legislation Committee eleventh, whereas interviews rank it fourth. The Government and Foreign Relations committees are placed at the top by Senate Rules, whereas senators rank them lower.

Senators and staff were asked why this discrepancy appeared. They

[9] Matthews, *U.S. Senators and Their World*, p. 152.

TABLE 23: Ranking of Senate Committees: Interviews versus Senate Rules

Ranking	Senators	Staff	Formal Rules
Most important			
1	Finance	Finance	Government
2	Constitution, Legislation, Justice, and Rules	Constitution, Legislation, Justice, and Rules	Foreign Relations
3	Government	Government	Constitution, Legislation, Justice, and Rules
4	Labor and Social Legislation	Labor and Social Legislation	Public Education
5	Foreign Relations	—	Finance
11	Mining	Economy and Commerce	Labor and Social Legislation
12	Interior Police	Public Health	Agriculture and Colonization
13	Economy and Commerce	Mining	Matters of Benefaction
14	Matters of Benefaction	Matters of Benefaction	Interior Police
Least important			

indicated that Article 29 is out of date and does not reflect recent trends. Numerous other objective indicators lend support to their ranking. One indicator is the number of committee reports issued. If a committee such as Finance meets regularly, works hard, and energetically exercises its gatekeeper role as provided by the Senate Rules, it would lend credence to interview response that places it at the top of Senate committees instead of fifth as per Article 29.

Examining Table 24, we see that for the period 1964–1967 the Finance Committee not only issued more reports than the Government Committee, which Article 29 places first (218 versus 191), but also reported thirty-three times with other committees while exercising its gatekeeper role over the annual budget. Similarly, the Constitution, Legislation, Justice, and Rules Committee (ranked second by senators) issued more reports than the Foreign Relations Committee (ranked

TABLE 24: Numbers of Standing Committee Reports, 1964–1967

Committee	1964	1965	1966	1967	Total
Finance[a]	59	51	69	39	218
Government	39	27	55	70	191
Constitution, Legislation, Justice, and Rules	—	—	26	41	67
Foreign Relations	—	—	15	37	52
Labor and Social Legislation	26	44	27	21	118
Economy and Commerce	2	6	4	6	18

SOURCE: Compiled from statistical bulletins issued by OIS during this period.

[a] Finance also reported jointly with other committees thirty-three times in the 1964–1967 period.

second by Article 29) or the Labor and Social Legislation Committee (ranked fourth by senators), and four times the number of reports as the Economy and Commerce Committee, which Article 29 ranked ahead of it (67 versus 18).

A second indicator is the number of years of congressional experience behind members on the top committees compared with members of the less important committees. Donald Matthews found that party leaders are concentrated in the elite committees in the U.S. Senate, and that the most senior members also served on the top committees.[10] No formal seniority system exists in the Chilean Senate. But, if we could demonstrate that senators with the longest congressional careers tended to serve on the top committees, and that they were important party leaders, it would suggest that more experienced senators tend to be recruited to the key committees, which reinforces the prestige these committees enjoy.

Calculating the average number of years served in Congress prior to assignment to committees in 1965, we see in Table 25 that members

[10] *Ibid.*, p. 151.

TABLE 25: Standing Committee Members' Years in Congress before Selection in 1965

	Avg. Yrs. in Congress of Members
Top five committees	
1. Finance	15.8
2. Constitution, Legislation, Justice, and Rules	10.2[a]
3. Government	15.6
4. Labor and Social Legislation	13.0
5. Foreign Relations	14.4
Avg. Total	13.8
Bottom two committees	
1. Mining	8.0
2. Economy and Commerce	5.6
Avg. total	6.8
Avg. total for all eight committees other than the top five	10.4[b]

[a] This Committee averages only 10.2 years because three members elected for the first time to the Senate in 1965 were placed on this Committee as the acknowledged experts in their respective parties on this subject area. Two of the three were also party floor leaders.

[b] One committee is not included (Matters of Benefaction); its membership is secret.

selected for the Finance Committee (interviews ranked first) had more years of congressional experience than for any other Senate committee (15.8 years). Furthermore, totaling the average number of years of congressional experience for the committees senators ranked as the top five, we see that the average total is 13.8 years versus only 10.4 years for all committees not in the top five. Also, when these totals are compared with those for Economy and for Commerce and Mining (two committee senators ranked as least important), we see that members of these two bottom committees have only 6.8 years of experience before assignment.

Many of the senators serving on the top five committees are also regarded as political party leaders. For example, Luis Bossay (PR) has been a presidential candidate for his party as well as a regular member of the Finance Committee for several years in both the Chamber and Senate. Ignacio Palma (PDC) and Julio Von Mühlenbrock (PN) were *comités* (floor leaders) in 1965. On the Constitution, Legislation, Justice, and Rules Committee, Fernando Alessandri (PN) was a former party presidential candidate (PL at the time), as well as president of the Senate for several years. In 1965, Patricio Aylwin was president of the Christian-Democrat party, Hermes Ahumada (PR) a member of the national party leadership, and Tomás Chadwick (PS) a floor leader.

A third indicator is the staff assistance for the top two committees of Finance and Constitution, Legislation, Justice, and Rules. These are the only two committees where the secretaries and assistants work exclusively on one committee and on no other. All other secretaries and assistants are responsible for two committees simultaneously.

A fourth indicator is the list of committee preferences presented by each bloc of political parties in 1965 when presidencies were allocated. Examination of unpublished minutes from interparty conferences of floor leaders in 1965 show that each of the two blocks—(1) National and Christian-Democrat parties, and (2) Socialist, Communist, National Vanguard of the People, and Independents—wished to chair the Finance Committee as their first choice. Furthermore, the bloc representatives (Palma and Ampuero) named as their first five preferences the same five committees senators specified in personal interviews.

Finally, a fifth indicator is scholarly works and Senate debates. For example, Jorge Tapia Valdés notes that the Finance and Government committees study a larger number of projects than the rest of the committees. He continues, "The intensity of work developed by the Committee of Government, of Labor and Social Legislation, and especially Finance is surprising."[11] Alejandro Silva Bascuñán states that Finance

---

[11] Jorge A. Tapia Valdés, *La técnica legislativa*, p. 30.

and Constitution, Legislation, Justice, and Rules are the two key committees,[12] and Carlos Andrade Geywitz argues that each party puts its best-prepared members on the committees of Constitution, Legislation, Justice, and Rules and Labor and Social Legislation.[13] In a revealing debate, independent socialist Senator Rafael Tarud complained that the Finance Committee traditionally encroaches on Economy and Commerce: "The truth is that the Senate hasn't given [the Committee of Economy and Commerce] the importance it should have, as is the fact, for example, for Government. . . . But, it has been traditional here, in the Senate, to give greater importance to the Finance Committee."[14]

CONCLUSION

Personal interviews (among senators and staff members) as well as analysis of other data (such as number of committee reports issued and membership stability) clearly indicate that there is a "pecking order" of standing committees in the Chilean Senate very similar to that identified by Donald R. Matthews in the U.S. Senate. The Finance Committee is regarded as the top committee by both senators and staff largely because of its formal and informal jurisdiction over both the financial and nonfinancial aspects of important bills, and the corresponding prestige and publicity membership on this committee affords. The specialized subject matter of this and the other top committees has encouraged committee members to adopt a nonpartisan manner in discussing bills, which is comparable to the style of the U.S. House Ways and Means Committee. Also significant is the fact that the ranking of committees appears to have varied over the years (particularly for the Labor and Social Legislation Committee), reflecting the Senate's institutional adaptation to new demands made by different sectors of the population as Chile has developed economically and politically.

---

[12] Alejandro Silva Bascuñán. *Tratado de derecho constitucional*, III, 175.

[13] Carlos Andrade Geywitz, *Elementos de derecho constitucional chileno*, pp. 444–446.

[14] *Diario de sesiones del senado, legislatura extraordinaria*, sesión 36a, April 12, 1961, pp. 2085–2086.

4. Recruitment and Stability of Committee Membership

SINCE CHILEAN SENATE COMMITTEES have jurisdiction over legislation that touches the interests of every political party, it is not surprising to find partisanship built into the allocation of committee seats and presidencies. As we shall see, the proportional allocation system used helps explain why opposition parties are capable of obstructing or modifying executive legislation. But what is significant in explaining the intermediate level of autonomy of committees as well as the Senate's capacity to form majority decisions across ideologically opposed political parties is the degree to which partisanship is muted in committees.

This phenomenon is linked to the nature of the recruitment process and the stability of committee membership. More specifically, recruitment is primarily a Senate party conference decision of all the senators (except for the Communist party) emphasizing criteria of expertise, specialization, personal preferences, constituency characteristics, and past committee service rather than one made by the national leadership of the various parties. Even when the national leadership exercises influence on recruitment, partisan considerations are counterbalanced by a desire to select senators who have demonstrated a capacity for cooperating and bargaining with other political parties. Also, the high level of membership stability on the two top committees of Finance and Constitution, Legislation, Justice, and Rules enables members to develop the specialized competence required to review executive legislation skillfully and to influence national party policy, and this is not materially affected by membership replacements within each four-year legislative period. A corollary is that the senators who most frequently influence their national party's policy stand (PN and PR) and sit on the top five committees also have the longest congressional careers.

ASSIGNMENT TO COMMITTEE BY PARTY BLOC OR INDIVIDUAL PARTY

Every four years (after congressional elections), standing committee membership is revised. According to Article 32 of the Senate Rules, the president of the Senate presents the list of membership, which the Senate as a whole elects.[1] In fact, the process works quite differently. The president simply establishes the number of seats on each committee for each party (or bloc, if parties act as a group) in mathematical proportion to its number of seats in the Senate.[2] By mutual agreement of the party floor leaders meeting with the president of the Senate, a modified formula may be adopted that maintains as closely as possible the proportional representation of seats as a whole, but alters it for specific committees. Allocating seats on committees to reflect relative party strength is comparable to the system used in the U.S. Congress. But, in Chile's multiparty system, where there is seldom if ever a majority party, this form of allocation may result in the government party's not being able to control the majority of the votes on committees.

---

[1] "Reglamento del senado" in *Manual del senado*, p. 123.
[2] Ingrid Ahumada Muñoz, *Las comisiones parlamentarias en Chile y otros países*, p. 62.

Even when it chairs a committee, its minority vote status severely limits the power of the president to push through government legislation and, as we have seen, enhances the opposition's capacity to obstruct or modify legislation.

Let us examine this process in more detail for the 1965–1969 legislative period. Following congressional elections in March, 1965, and the opening of the regular session of the Senate in May, the various party floor leaders met with the president of the Senate to determine the proportion of committee seats for each party.

Interviews and analysis of unpublished transcripts of floor leaders' meetings (*actas*) reveal that a mathematical formula strictly proportional to each party's strength in the Senate was not adopted.[3] In the 1965 congressional election campaign, the National Vanguard, National Democrat, Socialist, and Communist parties, along with some independents, acted as a bloc of the Left. The floor leaders for each of these parties decided to vote together in allocating committee seats so as to increase their bargaining weight. The Christian-Democrat, United Conservative, and Liberal parties (the last two parties of this group later joined to form the National party) responded in kind by joining to represent the Center-Right, while the Radical party remained neutral. Senator Aniceto Rodríguez (Socialist party) argued that each bloc would be most equitably represented on each committee, numerically and ideologically, if two of each of the total five seats were allocated to his leftist bloc, two for the center-right bloc, and one to the neutral Radical party. Tables 26 and 27 outline the distribution of seats by committee as adopted.

The use of this party-bloc apportionment system in a multiparty system denies the government party (PDC) not only a percentage of seats on committees equal to its Senate seats (20% versus 27%) but also, and more importantly, a majority on even one committee. Frequently, Radical senators vote with the leftist bloc to form a majority. Therefore, even when a government party senator chairs a committee, he may be overruled or even censured. This may severely restrict the accepted bounds of behavior of a Christian-Democrat president, and it

---

[3] *Actas de la sesión de los comités parlamentarios celebrada el dia 1 de Julio y 2 de Julio de 1965.*

TABLE 26: Committee Seat Distribution by Party Bloc, 1965–1969

Method of Distribution	Left PC, PS, VNP, PADENA, I	Neutral PR	Center-Right PDC, PL, PCU	Total Seats
Mathematical formula	25	14	31	70
Formula adopted	28	14	28	70

helps to explain why the government has such difficulty pushing legislation through the Senate. Accordingly, a premium is placed on the ability to bargain for concessions with opposition parties either in committee when specific articles and amendments are studied, or on the floor, or in interparty conferences of floor leaders.

The use of this bloc system may also affect whether a committee report is likely to be accepted on the Senate floor. Richard Fenno found that one of the ingredients to the successful passage of House Appropriations Committee reports on the floor was the ability of the committee to anticipate the mood or temper of the House in its reports and to represent its views.[4] Standing committees' success on the floor of the Chilean Senate also depends on their ability to represent the majority sentiment of the body. But, as Tables 26 and 27 show, one result of this system is that, although each bloc is represented on all committees, an important party within each bloc may not be (e.g., Communist party on Government). The committee may consciously work over a bill and the majority (though not of the floor) report out favorably, only to be defeated on the floor because the committee excludes a key party and therefore does not represent majority sentiment.

ASSIGNMENT OF COMMITTEE PRESIDENCIES
BY PARTY BLOC

Party floor leaders also work out agreements on how many committee presidencies will go to each party or bloc of parties and what spe-

---

[4] Richard F. Fenno, Jr., *The Power of the Purse: Appropriations Politics in Congress*, pp. 449–471.

TABLE 27: Specific Committee Seat Distribution by Bloc and by Party, 1965–1969

Committee	PC	PS	VNP, PADENA, I	PR	PDC	PL, PCU	Total Seats
		Left		Neutral	Center-Right		
Government	—	1	1	1	1	1	5
Foreign Relations	1	1	—	1	1	1	5
Constitution, Legislation, Justice, and Rules	—	1	1	1	1	1	5
Public Education	1	1	—	1	1	1	5
Finance	1	1	—	1	1	1	5
Economy and Commerce	—	1	1	1	1	1	5
National Defense	1	1	—	1	1	1	5
Public Works	1	1	—	1	1	1	5
Mining	1	1	—	1	1	1	5
Public Health	1	1	—	1	1	1	5
Labor and Social Legislation	1	1	—	1	1	1	5
Agriculture and Colonization	1	1	—	1	1	1	5
Interior Police	1	1	—	1	1	1	5
Matters of Benefaction	1	1	—	1	1	1	5
Subtotal	11	14	3	14	14	14	70
Bloc totals		28		14	28		70

[a] United Conservative and Liberal parties later united to form the National Party.

cific committees each will chair. Normally the number of seats allocated to each bloc or party is proportional to its strength in the Senate. But in 1965 the assignment of presidencies took an unusual twist. The

Radical party made an unprecedented decision not to accept the presidencies of any committees. They had emerged from the preceding presidential and congressional elections with the unfavorable image of wheeling and dealing with any party, regardless of its ideological position, in order to win votes. Under the influence of Senator Humberto Enríquez, who was then president of the national party as well, the party sought to improve its public image by refusing to bargain with other political parties in order to obtain some Senate committee presidencies. This neutral status left all the presidencies to be divided between the center-right and leftist blocs mentioned above.

By floor leader agreement, a drawing (*sorteo*) was conducted to determine which of the two party blocs would have the first choice, to opt between selecting the president of the committee they most wanted to chair (and every other choice thereafter) *or*, instead, chairing a total of seven versus six of the total fourteen standing committees. Senator Ampuero (PS), representing the Left, and Senator Palma (PDC), the Center-Right, met for the draw. Ampuero won and elected to take the presidency of the committee of his bloc's first choice, Finance, and every other choice thereafter.

Table 28 summarizes the bloc allocation of committee presidencies for the 1965–1969 legislative period. Although this arrangement determined the number of presidencies for each bloc, it did not determine which political party within each bloc would chair each committee. For these purposes, the Socialist, Communist, Liberal, and United Conservative parties voted in opposition to the government party (PDC), with the Radical party remaining neutral. Since these opposition parties controlled three of five votes in each committee, they could control the naming of the president within the limits of the six-seven bloc agreement. Accordingly, the two main parties within the leftist bloc (PS and PC) divided their six chairs equally with the supporting votes of the United Conservative and Liberal parties. In exchange, they voted in support of the United Conservative and Liberal parties' candidates on six of the seven center-right committees. The government party (PDC) agreed to the bloc arrangement, even though it underrepresented their weight in terms of senate seats, in return for the presidency of the second most important committee—Constitution, Legisla-

TABLE 28: Distribution of Committee Presidencies by Bloc and by Party, 1965–1969

Committee	Senator	Party
Left Bloc		
Finance	Altamirano	PS
National Defense	Ampuero	PS
Labor and Social		
Legislation	Contreras T.	PC
Mining	Contreras L.	PC
Public Education	Teitelboim	PC
Public Health	Allende	PS
Center-Right Bloc		
Government	Bulnes	PCU
Constitution, Legislation,		
Justice, and Rules[a]	Prado	PDC
Foreign Relations	Sepúlveda	PL
Public Works	Von Mühlenbrock	PL
Agriculture and		
Colonization	Curti	PCU
Economy and Commerce	Ibáñez	PL
Matters of	(secret)	
Benefaction		(secret)

SOURCE: Actas de los comités, July 1–2, 19, 1965.

[a] When the Special Committee on Constitutional Reform was set up in 1966, the Christian-Democrats received the presidency in deference to the fact that constitutional reform was a major plank of the executive's program. In return, the Socialist party obtained the presidency of Constitution, Legislation, Justice, and Rules.

tion, Justice, and Rules—and the presidency of the Senate, which usually goes to the majority bloc of parties in the Chamber.

One other key problem arose. As noted above, the leftist bloc divided its six committee presidencies equally between the Socialist and Communist parties. One of the Communist party's selections was Foreign Relations, and Communist Senator Teitelboim was named as the party candidate. But a Liberal senator strongly objected to a Communist senator chairing this committee. The president of the Foreign Relations Committee is often called on to represent Chile at diplomatic functions at home and abroad, and it was feared that his election would have an unfavorable impact internationally, particularly in the United States. Witness some excerpts from unpublished minutes of an interparty floor leader meeting:

The Honorable Senator Teitelboim wishes to record his rejection of the opinion that was manifested by one Senator establishing a veto principle to prevent the Communist party from entering certain committees.

The Honorable Senator Jaramillo explains that Senator Sepúlveda, Liberal party member of Foreign Relations, has not opposed the possibility that Senator Teitelboim will be designated president of this committee, and that in fact he was disposed to vote for him; but the real problem is rooted in the impossibility of completing in this committee the agreement that exists over the matter.[5]

A compromise solution was finally reached whereby Senator Teitelboim would receive the presidency of Public Education Committee in exchange for Foreign Relations, and Liberal Senator Sepúlveda was subsequently elected president of that committee.

RECRUITMENT TO COMMITTEES: ROLE OF
NATIONAL PARTY AND SENATE FLOOR LEADERS

Since each political party or bloc is represented on each Senate committee, one might expect to find deliberations plagued by the sharp partisan conflict that inhibits interparty agreements on important legislation. It is significant that committees serve instead as an arena for interparty accommodation and agreement. In part, this phenomenon may be explained by the nature of the recruitment process and the stability of membership on key committees.

First of all, senator and staff interviews indicate that recruitment to committees is primarily a Senate party conference decision of all the senators (except for the Communist party), based on criteria of expertise, specialization, personal preference, constituency characteristics,

---

[5] *Actas de la sesión de los comités parlamentarios celebrada el dia 19 de Julio de 1965.*

and past committee service, criteria which supersede the national party leaderships' partisan considerations. This statement should be amended, however, to note that, when disputes arise among senators over party seats, the party floor leaders may arbitrate. Furthermore, in certain cases the executive committee or council of each party or their floor leaders may designate party members on a Senate committee. For the Communist party, senator preferences and experience are considered, but the allocation of seats is the decision of the national party leadership.

Senators were asked, "Once the number of seats for each political party on standing committees is determined after an election (e.g., 1965), how does your party determine which senators will work on each of the respective committees?" All but two (forty-two) senators responded. Of these, every senator but the Communists noted that recruitment is a Senate conference decision. A typical comment was, "We usually reach a mutual accord among ourselves—after a while, there is a certain spirit [*ánimo*] about who should serve on each committee." For the Communist senators, the procedure differs: "The national party asks which committee we would like to serve on, and then a decision is reached based on one's capacity, other party duties, and enthusiasm." There is no committee on committees for each party, as in the U.S. Senate. Since the Chilean Senate is less than half the size of the U.S. Senate, and party senators number a maximum of twelve, a conference of all party senators led by the elected floor leaders can effectively meet informally to decide who will serve on each committee. In the case of Communist senators, a similar conference is held where senator preferences are discussed and transmitted either by the party president or floor leader to the national party leadership for final decision.

Interviews, an analysis of senators' occupational backgrounds, and a review of scholarly works also indicate that all parties emphasize such factors as a senator's expertise and previous experience when recruiting committee members.[6] For example, each party has its acknowledged experts in each field, who are generally appointed to the corresponding

---

[6] See, for example, Carlos Andrade Geywitz, *Elementos de derecho constitucional*, pp. 442–446.

subject matter committee—for example, Altamirano (PS) and Bossay (PR) on the Finance Committee or Aylwin (PDC) and F. Alessandri (PN) on Constitution, Legislation, Justice, and Rules. This procedure enhances specialized review of bills and amendments, which enables senators not only to confront government ministers with factual arguments when they appear before committees, but also to influence national party policy as well.

A similar practice encourages specialized study and expertise by allowing a senator to remain on a committee he is qualified for as long as he wishes to stay. For example, Salvador Allende (PS), president of the Senate and a doctor, has long been interested in public health problems and has regularly served on Public Health. It is unlikely that he would be easily removed by his party under normal circumstances.

Constituency characteristics also have a bearing on a senator's assignment or preference. For example, Humberto Aguirre Doolan (PR) seeks assignment on Agriculture and Colonization not only because he is an agricultural engineer, but also because his district is highly rural. Mining's importance in Hugo Miranda's (PR) and Tomás Chadwick's (PS) district helps explain why they sit on Mining. Simple member preference, wherever it can be accommodated, is another factor. Renán Fuentealba (PDC) is particularly interested in foreign relations and Chile's role in the world community. This indicated interest along with regular party service carried him on to the fifth-ranked committee.

An informal seniority system also appears to have developed in the Radical party for obtaining a seat on the key Finance Committee. The effect is probably to dampen still further partisan considerations in recruitment. One Radical senator explains: "I went on National Defense in 1953 when I first came to the Senate because Finance was occupied by other senators. Now Baltra would like to sit regularly on Finance, but he is just the *cola* [end of the line] behind Bossay, Durán, and Aguirre." Another Radical senator confirms this system: "Yes—there certainly is a period of waiting before you get a seat on Finance. I started out on a committee of minor importance in the Chamber, but then I moved up to Finance. . . . You establish your reputation here by action and years of service." Although Christian-Democrat senators did not specify whether they use similar criteria, there is some evidence to suggest that they do. For example, in 1965 at least four Christian-Democrat senators sought to fill their seat on Finance—Ignacio Palma, Rafael Gumucio, Tomás Pablo, and José Musalem. It was finally decided to rotate the seat among the senators—each to serve one year. But Palma, who had the greatest number of years in Congress, sat first. We might conclude that, although the number of years in Congress is not formally totaled and used as a legitimate claim to a key seat by these two parties, if all other qualifications of the candidates are equal (they often are not), senators are expected to show deference to the senator with the longest congressional career and to allow him to take the party seat on a key committee.

When the national party leadership or floor leaders exercise influence over Senate party conference decisions on recruitment (e.g., arbitrate a dispute over who should have the party seat on the Finance Committee), they seek to build partisanship into key committees by placing senators who are capable of defending the ideological position of the party. But, at the same time, they seek to insure that partisanship is handled in a fairly harmonious way by recruiting reasonable, moderate men who have a demonstrated capacity to cooperate with other political parties.

Recruitment to Finance, the Chilean Senate's most important committee, is a good example. The committee's jurisdiction over controversial, potentially partisan issues—such as the 1968 Salary Readjustment Bill, which called for public employees' salary adjustments by a lower percentage than the actual inflation over the preceding year (1967)—makes it a prime arena for intense partisan conflicts. Accordingly, each party seeks to place a member on the committee who is both an expert on economic matters and a representative of the sentiment of the majority of the party. If a choice is required between the two criteria, preference will be given to the latter. One senator succinctly described the process: "On Finance, we try to designate senators who are representative of the party at the time, with clear political positions, knowledge, and experience."

But every party recognizes that legislation that passes through this committee touches the interests not only of their party, but of the nation as well. Ideological hard lines and partisanship are expected, but only up to a point. Therefore, parties also tend to place on this committee their more experienced senators who have demonstrated a capacity to cooperate with other party leaders, especially when overriding national interests are involved.

STABILITY OF COMMITTEE MEMBERSHIP

When membership on a committee is relatively stable and continuous, members are able to develop their competence in the subject matter of the committee, which in turn may serve as a base of autonomous power.[7] Furthermore, a stable membership increases the probability that a set of internal norms and techniques for the resolution of potentially disruptive partisan conflict will be developed.[8] Therefore, if we could determine that top Chilean Senate committees were characterized by a stable and continuous membership over time, it would give us another variable for explaining how partisanship is contained (or dampened) in Senate committees and how this process is linked to their relative influence in the Senate system.

Analysis of the membership of the two top-ranked Chilean Senate committees, Finance and Constitution, Legislation, Justice, and Rules, for the period 1894–1965 clearly indicates a high level of continuity and stability over time. Table 29 shows that at least two (40%) or three (60%) of the total membership (five) continue from one four-year legislative period to the next, and at times four (80%) or the total committee do so (e.g., 1945–1949, 1957–1961). Furthermore, many senators have served *together* on the same committee for several periods. For example, from 1953 to 1965 Fernando Alessandri, Humberto Alvarez, and Francisco Bulnes served together on the Constitution, Legislation, Justice, and Rules Committee. On Finance, Eduardo Frei, Angel Faivovich, and Gregorio Amunátegui worked together from 1953 to 1961. Frequently, a senator will also have served on the same standing committee in the Chamber and later in the Senate. For example, Senator Bulnes served from 1945 to 1953 on Constitution,

---

[7] Fenno, *The Power of the Purse*, pp. 57–60.

[8] Richard F. Fenno, Jr., "The Appropriations Committee as a Political System," in *New Perspectives on the House of Representatives*, ed. Robert L. Peabody and Nelson W. Polsby, p. 89.

TABLE 29: Membership Continuity on Senate Committees of Finance and Constitution, Legislation, Justice, and Rules, 1894–1965

	% Membership Continuing	
	Constitution, Legislation, Justice, and Rules Committee	Finance Committee
1894–1897	60	40
1897–1900	100	40
1900–1903 (March)	20	60
1900–1903 (April)	60	100
1903–1906	80	80
1906–1909	20	60
1909–1912	40	100
1912–1915	20	60
1915–1918	60	100
1918–1921	60	80
1921–1924	100	80
1924	60	40
1926–1930	40	40
1930–1932	80	80
1933–1937	20	0
1937–1941	60	100
1941–1945	80	40
1945–1949	80	100
1949–1953	60	80
1953–1957	60	60
1957–1961	80	60
1961–1965	60	20

SOURCE: Compiled from data in Luis Valencia Avaria, *Anales de la república*, vols. 1 and 2.

Legislation, Justice, and Rules (one of the two most important committees) while in the Chamber. Elected to the Senate, he served on the same committee from 1953 to 1965. Senator Bossay served on the Finance Committee in the Chamber from 1949 to 1953 and in the Senate from 1965 to 1969. Fernando Alessandri, whose entire career has been in the Senate, has worked on Constitution, Legislation, Justice, and Rules continuously since 1937.

It is important to note, however, that this hard core of membership stability has historically been concentrated in the center-right parties (PCU, PL, PR).[9] This in turn explains, in part, our earlier findings that senators who are members of these parties tend to exercise more influence than senators from other parties on the formation of national party policy.

This fact is demonstrated when we control the current Senate membership (1968) for party. Table 30 clearly shows that Radical and National (formally the Liberal and United Conservative parties) senators have served an average of 16.4 and 13.8 years in Congress as of 1965, compared with only 7.0, 8.8, and 11.7 years for the Christian-Democrats, Communists, and Socialists, respectively. As we saw earlier, parties tend to place their most experienced senators, also generally their greatest experts on specific subjects, on the top five committees. Therefore, if the Radical and National parties have a corner on the number of senators with long career experience, we would expect that this would be less so for these five committees than any others. Even though this is true, we still find (see Table 31) that the average number of years in Congress for National and Radical senators on the Finance Committee is 18.0 versus 14.3 for Christian-Democrat, Socialist, and Communist senators, and 25.5 versus zero on Constitution, Legislation, Justice, and Rules. This holds true for the remaining three committees in the top five as well: Government, 18.0 versus 12.0; Labor and Social Legislation, 16.0 versus 9.7; and Foreign Relations, 18.0

---

[9] This is a direct product of the partial, off-year election of the Senate. Chile, like France, has seen in its recent history the rise and fall of numerous "flash" parties as well as independent, nonparty movements led by charismatic presidential candidates (e.g., Ibáñez in 1952). The election system for the Senate has to a certain degree insulated it from these periodic tides, thereby enabling the predominant parties during the 1891–1961 period (United Conservatives, Liberals, and Radicals) to build up a certain measure of member stability, comparable with that of the U.S. Senate. This membership stability was not built up in the Communist party because of the Law for the Defense of Democracy, which outlawed the party from 1948 to 1958. This situation and corrupt electoral practices in the first quarter of the twentieth century have favored (until 1961) the center-right group of political parties.

TABLE 30: Years of Congressional Experience
for Senators by Major Party, 1965

	PC	PS	PDC	PR[a]	PN[b]
	4	24	0	16	31
	27	4	0	20	20
	5	12	12	0	4
	4	14	8	24	12
	4	0	8	20	12
		16	8	16	
			12	8	
			0	24	
			8	20	
			12	16	
			0		
			16		
Total	44	70	84	164	79
Avg. Yrs.	8.8	11.7	7.0	16.4	13.8

SOURCE: Compiled from Library of Congress Biographical Data Project File.

[a] Maurás, now a member of the National party, was a Radical in 1965, and is included there.

[b] Sepúlveda, now an independent, was a member of the Liberal party in 1965, which later became a part of the National party, and is included there.

versus 8.0. When the average years in Congress for each group are totaled for all five top committees, the comparative figures are 19.1 versus 8.8.

The most startling example is the Constitution, Legislation, Justice, and Rules Committee. Fernando Alessandri (PN) and Hermes Ahumada (PR) have served, respectively, thirty-one and twenty years in Congress. Both Alessandri and Ahumada have been presiding officers in either the Chamber or the Senate. Alessandri had the experience of two decades of committee work, where precedents were laid for interpreting not only the Constitution, but the Senate Rules as well. This warehouse of congressional and committee experience must enable them to influence committee work far beyond their numerical weight.

TABLE 31: Years of Congressional Experience for Senators on Top Five Committees, 1965

	Total Years for Each Senator by Party								
	Center-Right					Center-Left			
Committee	PC	PS	VNP, PADENA	PDC	Total Avg.	PR	PN[a]	Total Avg.
Finance	27	4	—	12	14.3	24	12	18.0
Constitution, Legislation, Justice, and Rules	—	0	0	0	0	20	31	25.5
Government	—	24.4	—	8	12.0	16	20	18.0
Labor and Social Legislation	5	16	—	8	9.7	20	12	16.0
Foreign Relations	4	—	12	8	8.0	20	16	18.0
Avg. Yrs.	12.0	9.6	6.0	7.3	8.8	20.0	18.2	19.1

SOURCE: Compiled from Congressional Records and Library of Congress Biographical Data Project File.

[a] Liberal and United Conservative parties formed the National Party.

Contrast their backgrounds with those of Senators Benjamín Prado (PDC), Tomás Chadwick (PS), and Luis Fernando Luengo (PADENA), the three other members of the committee. Each is certainly an expert in the subject matter of the committee, and Chadwick in particular has a reputation as an outstanding lawyer. But each was newly elected to the Senate in 1965, and is hence a greenhorn to this committee. In time, they probably will gain a level of experience comparable to Alessandri and Ahumada, but for the moment it is questionable whether they carry as much weight as the more experienced members.

Jorge Tapia Valdés suggests that, even when membership stability exists on committees for many years, a custom of replacing a regular party member several times during a legislative period (four years) detrimentally affects members' ability to become specialists in the matters the committee reviews.[10]

If intraparty turnover regularly occurs on committees during a legislative period, as Tapia indicates, the process may not only be significant in terms of its impact on members' ability to specialize. It may also indicate that committees act as agents of national political parties on some issues and have independent influence on others. Or committee membership replacement may simply reflect other phenomena, such as fulfillment of normative expectations that a regular member will step down while a party colleague's pet project passes through committee.

Since intra-legislative-period turnover on committees had not been anticipated, I fortunately came across Tapia's quotation *before* interviews actually began. Two subsequent steps were taken: (1) location of objective indicators to verify empirically whether replacement as described does occur and, if so, how often, controlling for party, and (2) addition of a question to our interview schedule that would help determine why and under what conditions replacement does occur.

Access was made available to unpublished Senate documents for all committees covering the period May 21, 1965 (start of regular session of legislative period), to May 20, 1968 (end of regular and extraordinary sessions). Data for the Finance Committee will be presented here. Beginning with the regular members named by each party for the leg-

---

[10] Jorge A. Tapia Valdés, *La técnica legislativa*, pp. 29–30.

islative period, replacements were traced until May 20, 1968. A total of sixty-seven replacements of the regular members occurred during this period, by party as follows: National, ten; Radical, twelve; Christian-Democrat, fourteen; Socialist, thirteen; Communist, eighteen. Of the total days the Senate was in session (regular and extraordinary sessions), regular committee members on Finance were replaced 37 percent of the time, by party as follows: National, 27 percent; Radical, 40 percent; Christian-Democrat, 29 percent; Socialist, 44 percent; Communist, 47 percent (see Tables 32–36). All replacements for this period were intra-party, except when Víctor Contreras (PC) sat for a few hours for a Socialist senator (Socialists and Communists form the leftist bloc of parties). Therefore, parties maintain the same proportional representation on the committee even though the senators attending sessions may not always be those originally named in any given period.

When senators were asked, "Why is replacement of members on standing committees so high?" the forty (91%) senators responding mentioned nine separate causes in order of frequency: district and foreign travel; another party senator's greater knowledge about a bill; sickness; ability to sit in on all sessions limited by number of senators each party has; bill may favor district of other party senator; party factors; other political responsibilities; election campaigns; and the fact that not all senators work in committees.

Each party seeks to assure that its seats are filled on committees as often as possible. Whenever the regular member is traveling to his district, for example, floor leaders fill the vacancy with another party member. Some parties find it particularly difficult to keep their seats filled, either because of the small number of senators they have or because of other political duties some members must perform. For example, Luis Corvalán is secretary general of the Communist party as well as a senator. Because of his former duties, he seldom works on committees. The Communist party has only five senators, and Carlos Contreras has frequently been ill. All this places a heavy burden on Communist Senators Víctor Contreras, Volodia Teitelboim, and Julieta Campusano, who must serve on several committees. If two of their committees are cited for the same hour, they could not possibly attend

TABLE 32: Replacements of Regular Finance Committee Members, May 21, 1965–May 20, 1968: National Party

Period Regular Members Von Mühlenbrock or Ibáñez Replaced	Replacement	Days Not in Committee
7/13/65–7/26/65	Sepúlveda	13
1/26/66–3/21/66	Jaramillo	51
11/29/66–12/7/6C	Sepúlveda	7
1/19/67–4/7/67	Sepúlveda	76
6/20/67–7/25/67	Bulnes/Sepúlveda[a]	34
11/28/67–1/2/68	Bulnes	34
1/23/68–1/25/68	Jaramillo	1
2/6/68–3/6/68	Jaramillo	27
4/18/68–4/19/68	Curti	1
4/29/68–5/30/68	Bulnes/Curti[a]	31
Total days not in committee[b]		268
		(27% available days)

SOURCE: Compiled from unpublished Senate documents.

[a] Two senators sat on Finance before one of the two regular members re-turned.

[b] Von Mühlenbrock and Ibáñez rotated two years each from 1965 to 1969 to resolve their dispute over the party seat. Calculations of replacement are based on when these two members were not on Finance.

both sessions. Under these circumstances, one regular member (e.g., Teitelboim) might be replaced by one of the other Communist senators who is not occupied at that time.

As discussed earlier, Chilean Senate committees enjoy somewhat less autonomy from party leadership than U.S. congressional committees. This is further substantiated by the fact that executive committees of national parties instigate some of the intralegislative period replacements that occur. Senators named political party reasons as one of the nine causes for replacement. On a limited number of major bills that clearly involve ideological commitments of the various parties (e.g., nationalization of copper production, agrarian reform), the executive committees of the national parties issue orders as to how members

TABLE 33: Replacements of Regular Finance Committee Members, May 21, 1965–May 20, 1968: Radical Party

Period Regular Member Bossay Replaced	Replacement	Days Not in Committee
8/10/65–10/7/65	Gómez	57
12/7/65–12/7/65	Gómez	0
12/29/65–1/10/66	Gómez	11
1/27/66–1/27/66	Gómez	0
7/19/66–7/28/66	Miranda	8
8/17/66–9/13/66	Miranda	26
11/15/66–4/11/67[a]	Miranda/Gómez/Miranda/ Juliet/González	146
4/25/67–5/9/67	Miranda	14
5/11/67–6/19/67	Aguirre	37
8/29/67–11/9/67	Miranda	71
2/27/68–3/6/68	Miranda	6
4/20/68–5/9/68	Miranda	9
Total days not in committee		395 (40% available days)

SOURCE: Compiled from unpublished Senate documents.

[a] Normally the regular member returns after one senator replaces him. For this period, five senators sat on Finance before Bossay returned on April 11, 1967.

should vote. Replacements may occur in two ways while these bills are being studied. One is when the regular member of a committee temporarily steps down if he feels in good conscience that he can not carry out the party orders. One Radical senator told of an instance when he did just that: "You can always ask another member to replace you to represent the party if you don't agree with the party stand. I did this on the Education Reform Bill. I thought it was wrong for the party to be opposed to the project in the Senate after our own deputies voted for it in the Chamber." Second, the president of the national party, if he is a senator, may replace the regular member temporarily if he feels this will dramatize the issue and secure publicity for the party's posi-

TABLE 34: Replacements of Regular Finance Committee Members, May 21, 1965–May 20, 1968: Christian-Democrat Party

Period Regular Members Palma, Gumucio, Pablo Replaced	Replacement	Days Not in Committee
4/20/66–5/20/66ᵃ	Noemi	30
7/15/66–7/28/66	Noemi	12
8/3/66–8/16/66ᵇ	Noemi/Ferrando	11
8/18/66–10/3/66	Ferrando	35
11/2/66–11/22/66ᵇ	Noemi/Ferrando	18
11/23/66–11/24/66	Noemi	1
11/29/66–12/1/66	Ferrando	2
12/16/66–12/22/66	Noemi	5
1/11/67–4/11/67ᵇ	Noemi/Gormaz	88
4/25/67–6/19/67	Ferrando	24
6/28/67–8/1/67	Noemi	32
11/13/67–11/20/67	Noemi	6
1/3/68–1/23/68	Aylwin	19
2/27/68–3/5/68	Prado	6

Total days not in committeeᶜ		289
		(29% available days)

SOURCE: Compiled from unpublished Senate documents.

ᵃ Note that for almost the first full year in power, no Christian-Democrat replacements were made (5/21/65–4/20/66) versus several by other parties. This appears to have been an attempt to guide government legislation through the committee.

ᵇ Two senators sat on Finance before one of the regular members returned.

ᶜ Palma, Gumucio, and Pablo rotated as regular members for one year each to resolve the Christian-Democrat dispute over who would fill the seat. Calculations of replacements are based on when these members are not on Finance.

tion. For example, it would appear that Miranda's (president of the Radical party) replacing Bossay on Finance on February 27, 1968, and April 20, 1968, served this purpose, since the controversial Salary Readjustment Bill was under study at that time (see Table 31). Finally, the party floor leader may also occasionally replace a member who is

TABLE 35: Replacements of Regular Finance Committee Members, May 21, 1965–May 20, 1968: Socialist Party

Period Regular Member Altamirano Replaced	Replacement	Days Not in Committee
6/10/65–6/14/65	Rodríguez	3
9/13/65–9/21/65	S. Corbalán	7
1/26/66–1/28/66	S. Corbalán	2
5/2/66–5/12/66	Ampuero	10
6/7/66–4/5/67[a]	S. Corbalán/Chadwick	301
4/12/67–5/8/67	Chadwick	25
5/9/67–6/19/67	Chadwick	39
8/1/67–8/22/67	Rodríguez	20
9/7/67–9/7/67	Allende	0
11/8/67–11/9/67[b]	Carrera	1
11/28/67–11/28/67	V. Contreras (PC)	0
1/28/68–2/5/68	Luengo	8
4/17/68–5/13/68	Carrera	25
Total days not in committee		441 (44% available days)

SOURCE: Compiled from unpublished Senate documents.

[a] Two senators sat on Finance before the regular member returned.

[b] Altamirano was sanctioned by the Supreme Court for statements against President Frei and the military, and served a short jail sentence. Rodríguez took his place for the balance of the period covered.

not working hard in committee or attending the sessions of the committee.

Earlier we noted that expertise and specialization in the concerns of the Finance Committee and Constitution, Legislation, Justice, and Rules Committee in part account for these committees' relative autonomy in the Senate system, and that the level of autonomy is likely to increase when there is a high continuity of membership. We found that membership on these two committees was quite stable from one legislative period to the next for the period 1894 to 1965. The ques-

TABLE 36: Replacements of Regular Finance Committee Members, May 21, 1965–May 20, 1968: Communist Party

Period Regular Member C. Contreras Replaced[a]	Replacement	Days Not in Committee
7/22/65–7/30/65	Teitelboim	7
8/10/65–8/24/65	Campusano	13
9/21/65–11/2/65	Campusano	42
11/9/65–11/15/65	Campusano/V. Contreras	5
1/3/66–1/25/66	Teitelboim/Campusano	21
3/22/66–3/24/66	V. Contreras	1
3/24/66–3/28/66	Teitelboim	3
3/29/66–4/4/66	V. Contreras	5
4/14/66–4/18/66	V. Contreras	3
4/19/66–6/11/66	V. Contreras	52
7/28/66–9/1/66	Teitelboim/L. Corvalán/Teitelboim	33
9/5/66–12/14/66	Teitelboim/V. Contreras/Teitelboim/ V. Contreras/L. Corvalán	109
5/11/67–7/11/67	Campusano/V. Contreras/ Campusano	59
7/11/67–8/3/67	V. Contreras	22
8/22/67–11/8/67	V. Contreras	77
11/20/67–11/22/67	V. Contreras	1
4/19/68–4/20/68	V. Contreras	1
4/22/68–5/17/68	V. Contreras	15
Total days not in committee		469 (47% available days)

SOURCE: Compiled from unpublished Senate documents.

[a] Normally, the regular member returns after one senator replaces him. For several periods, two or three senators sat on Finance before C. Contreras returned. In part, this may be explained by prolonged illness of the regular member.

tion now is whether replacements within a legislative period weaken our findings.

Detailed analysis of replacements on Finance from May 21, 1965, to May 20, 1968, plus senator and staff interviews show that, although specialization may be reduced somewhat by the process of membership replacements during each four-year legislative period in Chile, the level is still quite high and comparable to that of top committees in the U.S. Senate. The U.S. senator is a busy man faced with many demands on his time that detract from his best intention to work hard, specialize, and study bills in committee. Mending fences in his district, for example, often may result in his absence from committee hearings or sessions. No one is there to replace him. In Chile a senator is faced with a similar dilemma, as evidenced by the senators' responses to why replacements occur. But, instead of leaving a vacant seat in committee, as in the United States, senators wherever possible replace members of their same party temporarily while the regular member is away or on other duties. Many of the replacements seen in Tables 32–36 may be attributed to this process.

The replacements that do occur often are not timed to have as great an impact on specialization as one might expect. Take, for example, Radical Senator Bossay (Table 31), a recognized expert in financial and business matters, who is also director or director-stockholder in several major companies started in 1965. Bossay was not in his seat for twelve periods, totaling 40 percent of committee time. But this should not be interpreted to mean that he missed 40 percent of the important bills considered. A senator and staff member point out: "There are not many changes while an important bill is being considered." "Members try to be there when an important bill is studied." Further research is necessary to determine fully what members actually miss during their absence, but the author's observations of Senate processes suggest they probably miss a smaller proportion of the important legislation than days absent would indicate.

Furthermore, when regular members are replaced, an attempt is made (barring national party influence) to call on senators in the party who possess similar qualifications: "We don't replace a member with just any senator if we can help it. For example, the Radical party might replace Senator Bossay with Baltra, or the Christian-Democrats Senator Palma with Gumucio." Data on Finance Committee replacements for each party lend some support to this statement (see Tables 32–36). For example, Senator Sergio Sepúlveda or Armando Jaramillo replaced the regular member for the National party 70 percent of the time, and they possess comparable qualifications. Senator Bossay of the Radical party was replaced nearly every time by Jonas Gómez or Hugo Miranda. Although it appears Tapia is correct to conclude that absence of a regular member reduces the degree of specialized study in committee, the effective level still remains quite high.

SUMMARY AND CONCLUSIONS

Partisanship is built into Senate committees through the use of an allocation system that distributes committee seats and presidencies in rough proportion to individual party or bloc (one or more parties) strength in the Senate. The practical effect of using this system in a multiparty environment like Chile is that it denies the government party (PDC) a majority on any Senate committee. Even when a Christian-Democrat chairs a committee, the fact that he lacks a majority makes it difficult to push legislation through the Senate. Also, the bloc system employed in 1965–1969 resulted in one important party's not being represented on two key committees, thereby increasing the likelihood that their reports might be rejected on the Senate floor.

What is interesting and significant in explaining the intermediate level of autonomy of committees as well as the Senate's capacity to form majority decisions across ideologically opposed political parties is the degree to which partisanship is effectively muted in committees. In addition to the explanations offered in previous chapters for this phenomenon, the nature of the recruitment process and stability of committee membership are explanatory variables. For example, Senate party conferences rather than the national party leadership primarily decide who will be recruited to each committee; such criteria as expertise, specialization, constituency characteristics, and past committee service are applied. Even when the national party leadership exercises influence (e.g., arbitrates disputes over seats), partisan considerations are counterbalanced by a desire to select senators who have demonstrated a capacity for cooperating and bargaining with other political parties. Norms of interparty cooperation and compromise, as well as member specialization, are further developed by a relatively stable and continuous membership on the two top committees, Finance and Constitution, Legislation, Justice, and Rules. Replacements within a legislative period do not appear to affect this relationship materially.

Finally, member stability on the top committees is concentrated in the National and Radical parties, which helps explain why these senators tend to exercise more influence on the national party leaderships than vice versa.

5. The Presidency of Standing Committees

WE HAVE SEEN SEVERAL INDICATORS suggesting that the presidency of a standing committee is not a very powerful role in the Chilean Senate. First of all, there is no seniority system that governs the selection process and prevents removal. Second, floor leaders of the political parties were able to determine in one instance who should chair a particular committee (Senator Sepúlveda on the Foreign Relations Committee). Third, the multiparty system and bloc apportionment of chairs increases the likelihood that senators will chair a committee on which they have little or no experience—perhaps even less than other members. Finally, the Radical party was prepared to give up its share of the presidencies of Senate committees in an attempt to improve the party image.

Still, this does not mean that the role of president is unimportant, or that some presidents do not enjoy considerable influence. To uncover the bases and scope of power of the presidency of Chilean Senate committees, we will employ an analytical framework consisting of five bases of power, which was used by John F. Manley to study the chairman of the U.S. House Ways and Means Committee:

1. *Legitimate power*: based on the norms and values associated with a person's role.
2. *Expert power*: based on a person's expertise and knowledge.
3. *Referent power*: based on having others identify with oneself.
4. *Reward power*: based on the ability to manipulate rewards for others.
5. *Negative power*: based on the ability to manipulate sanctions for others.[1]

LEGITIMATE POWER

The legitimate authority ascribed to the presidency of a Chilean Senate committee is based on a group of formal prerogatives similar to those held by chairmen of U.S. congressional committees.[2] Interviews suggest, however, that the ability to use these prerogatives as a base of power may be somewhat more limited.

We sought to tap senators' perceptions of the role of president by asking, "Is the presidency of a committee a powerful position or only symbolic?" Ninety-five percent (forty-two) of the senators responded. The great majority of the senators (88%, or thirty-seven) interjected a middle range of terms to define their views of the role, such as "important" or "important but not powerful." Five chose to describe the role as powerful, and only one replied that it was merely symbolic (see Table 37).

Interview comments by two senators who had visited the U.S. Senate or were familiar with its functioning were particularly useful for comparative purposes. Said one, "Well, I would say that the power of

---

[1] John F. Manley, "The House Committee on Ways and Means: 1947–1966" (Ph.D. dissertation, Syracuse University, 1967), p. 112.

[2] "Reglamento del senado," in *Manual del senado*, pp. 123–127; see Malcolm E. Jewell and Samuel C. Patterson, *The Legislative Process in the United States*, pp. 223–224.

TABLE 37: Senators' Description of Role of Standing Committee Presidents

Powerful, very powerful	4
Evidently important, very important, of great importance, fundamental	3
Important, important but not powerful	25
Not very important, of certain importance, of limited importance, not decisive, more than symbolic	9
Symbolic	1
No answer	2
Total	44

a president is more than formal, but certainly less than that of the chairmen of your committees." The other added, "The president has a number of formal prerogatives just as the president of the Senate does, but even so, he is not as important as one of your chairmen—say Senator Fulbright."

The five most frequently named prerogatives were: (1) to regulate when and how often committee meetings will be held, (2) to set the agenda for non-urgency bills, (3) to direct the debate, (4) to declare amendments to a bill offered in committee inadmissable when they have no relation to the basic or fundamental idea of a bill, and (5) to declare amendments to a bill offered in committee unconstitutional. Taken as a whole, they offer the president the potential to determine how a committee will work. Apparently, a president (along with the secretary) may be the only one fully aware of all the bills ready for review by a committee. This places him in a position to influence what the committee will consider first after executive urgency legislation. One committee secretary states: "Members generally don't know all the bills that are up for consideration. A president can say, 'Oh, this bill is not very important; let's consider it later.' " As a result, some bills may get shifted to the bottom and never come up for consideration. Strict interpretation of the admissibility or unconstitutionality of an amendment can affect whether pet projects will be attached to key legislation. Notes one staff member, "When the Salary Readjustment Bill went through the Senate, the president ruled six hundred of the two thousand proposed amendments inadmissible."

The number of sessions the president calls and how effectively he directs debates can determine the total rhythm of the work of a committee. One senator noted: "A president can certainly do a lot to speed up committee work. Just the number of committee sessions he calls can have a big impact on what we get done." Another said: "The way a president runs debates is important. If he really studies a bill and comes in and informs members, states his views, and tells members which articles to watch out for, like Fernando Alessandri used to do, senators can vote yes or no on the basis of his views. This gives the president influence. But, if he comes in and just says, 'I offer the floor,' you get a lot of views, slower work, and sometimes complete chaos."

Two variables set limitations on how and to what degree a president may exercise these formal prerogatives. The first is a set of norms that define how a president should perform his role.[3] Time permitted asking one-half (twenty-two) of the senators interviewed this question: "What role ought a committee president to play in order to be more effective in his job?" Responses across political parties specified a cluster of three norms: impartiality, democratic demeanor, and tolerance.

One-half (eleven) of these senators mentioned the first norm. Members expect the president of a committee to be an instrumental leader— to fix the calendar, call witnesses, and lead debates. But this style should be nonpartisan. Presidents are respected if they avoid twisting Senate Rules to a particular party's or bloc's advantage, guiding debates with an eye to the national interest. One senator exclaimed, "He should direct debates, participate actively, cite the interested parties on a bill, but he also should observe the rules and avoid political games." Another senator added, "He has the same obligations as the president of the Senate—to respect the rights of all the political parties."

[3] Role theory states that each role reflects agreed-upon expectations as to how members holding key positions should behave. Each role in turn is defined by a cluster of norms. For a discussion of this concept, see John W. Thibaut and Harold H. Kelley, *The Social Psychology of Groups*, p. 148. For examples of legislative research employing role theory, see Richard F. Fenno, Jr., *The Power of the Purse: Appropriations Politics in Congress*; John C. Wahlke *et al.*, *The Legislative System: Explorations in Legislative Behavior.*

Slippage occasionally occurs, but, in the main, presidents observe this norm. One apparently pleased senator exclaimed, "Most have presided impartially even though they had been active politicians before." Why? Senators know that five different parties chair Senate committees. Highly partisan behavior on the part of one could set off a chain reaction of partisanship among all the committees or could lead to member censure of the president.

This norm is reinforced by a nonpartisan staff. Unlike the U.S. system, where committee staffs are frequently divided along party lines, the Chilean Senate committee staff is available to the total committee. Staff members are recruited on the basis of competitive exam and advance through seniority and merit. Staff jobs are not dependent on the fortunes of political parties or personal loyalties to the president, as is frequently the case in the U.S. Senate.[4]

The second norm, democratic demeanor (named by 46%, or ten of the respondents), is closely linked to the first. The president is expected to be democratic, not authoritarian, in the performance of his instrumental tasks. Senators take great pride in the fact that they generally improve bills sent over by the Chamber, and much of this work is accomplished in committees. But bills can be improved and legitimized only in an environment where a democratic exchange of viewpoints is assured. Hence, a president is supposed to be "cooperative," "not pretentious," "flexible," "restrained," and "reasonable" when exercising his prerogatives. For example, if a member asks that a particular witness be cited for hearings on a bill, the president is expected to cite him. If a member wants to make his views heard on a particular article, the president is expected to give him the floor.

The third norm, named by 45 percent (ten) of the respondents, is tolerance. As we noted initially, the executive often tags his legislation urgent, and the bills must then be placed at the top of a committee's calendar. By the time these and a few other bills are passed, the Senate session may be over. Therefore, an informal practice has developed whereby senators attach their pet legislation in the form of amendments to an urgent bill, whether it has any relationship to the

4 Donald R. Matthews, *U.S. Senators and Their World*, p. 160.

bill or not. If presidents were to interpret Senate Rules strictly and to declare that these amendments are inadmissible because they are not germane to the subject matter of the bill, virtually no Senate bills would be passed at all. Accordingly, a president is expected to restrain his use of this prerogative. Said one senator: "The president has to accept a certain number of these amendments. There is a certain amount of tolerance [*Hay cierta tolerencia*]." If in doubt on how to rule on a particular amendment, the president is expected to exercise Article 101 of the Senate Rules, which allows him to consult the total committee or even to raise the matter on the floor. A representative comment was, "A president shouldn't try to act like a king and push a doubtful decision down our throats."

A second variable that may set even more severe restrictions on the president's use of his formal prerogatives is whether he has the backing of a majority in his committee. In the U.S. Congress, one party always has a majority of the seats, and chairmen of all committees are members of that party. On key issues, they normally count on their majority party's support. The situation is markedly different in the Chilean Senate. As a result of the party bloc arrangement in 1965, five different parties chaired committees. In some committees, a president may have to contend with a majority bloc of opposing parties, and even when he represents the majority, it is a bloc of several parties that may divide on any particular issue. Nor do presidents enjoy the same degree of autonomy as chairmen of U.S. committees. Although it is not a frequent occurrence, a president may be censured and removed by a majority vote of his committee.

One-third of the senators offered specific examples of how an opposing majority may limit a president's action. Normally, the president makes up the committee calendar and sets the agenda for sessions. But a majority of the members can vote to add a bill to the calendar. If a president is trying to push a piece of legislation the majority opposes, they may ask to call witnesses antagonistic to the bill, arrive late to committee sessions, or even refuse to attend at all. The president may attempt to retaliate by declaring inadmissible amendments that members of the majority (singly or jointly) are interested in, but then a majority can always resort to censure. Normally, open partisan-

ship does not reach these levels in committees (versus the floor). The
government party knows that in a multiparty environment votes from
opposing parties are necessary for passage of their bills and vice-versa.
In exchange terms, at the committee level, members are prepared to
allow the president considerable leeway in forming the calendar, in
making the agenda, and in calling sessions. They will even allow the
president to declare certain amendments inadmissible. But they expect
to get something in return.[5] By observing the norms mentioned above,
members can feel a part of the group. They know they will be able to
speak their piece. At the very least, many of their amendments will be
attached to urgency bills, and this may help their re-election. One
minority president described the relationship this way: "The overall
spirit in this committee is tolerance. I'm working against the current
all the time. The other members can hold me up in a lot of ways. So,
we just have a lot of give and take, compromise, and get things done."

EXPERT POWER

One of the several norms senators use to define the role of president
of a committee is expertise in the subject matter of the committee.
Thirty-nine percent (seventeen) of the senators specifically mentioned
that a president is more effective in his work and has the greater respect of his colleagues if he is master of the subject matter and bills
in his committee.

Clearly, some presidents fulfill these expectations better than others,
and this explains why they enjoy more influence in their committee.
Several senators noted this connection. One said, "If the president is
well versed on a bill, he is *the senator* of the committee." A second
senator added, "A president's importance largely depends on whether
or not he knows the subject he is talking about." For those presidents
who lack a majority for support, this base of power may provide a
means of communication that transcends partisan differences and leads
to a common ground for agreement.

An experienced staff member who had worked with several presi-

---

[5] For a discussion of the processes of exchange relationships, see Peter M. Blau,
Exchange and Power in Social Life, especially ch. 4.

dents over the past two decades recalled the influence Senator Bossay (PR)) exercised when he was president of Finance:

A president has more influence if he has a good knowledge of the subject matter of the committee. He can really sway the majority vote. Take Bossay. The positions he took the majority generally did too. Now the current president has very little experience. I've noticed that the committee work depends directly on the type of president you have. The members respect technical knowledge.

When a president combines expertise with experience, skill, and an agreeable style, his views may have a tremendous impact on a committee's decisions. Fernando Alessandri was such a president on Constitution, Legislation, Justice, and Rules. Exposed to politics early in life, he sat at the side of his father, Arturo Alessandri, when the Constitution of 1925 was written. Formally trained in constitutional law and with several years of teaching experience behind him, Alessandri entered the Senate in 1934 as a recognized expert in his field. Service on the same committee for several decades provided an accumulation of experience unparalleled in Senate history. Active in writing numerous committee reports that set the precedent for current committee action, he is a living library of knowledge in this field. Blessed by a gracious manner, he was the epitome of what a good president should be. Fair and respectful to all the members, he dominated sessions not by brute force, but by knowledge. Able to draw on the experience of having personally attended the sessions that drafted the Constitution of 1925, Alessandri would carefully weave his argument for this or that interpretation with uncommon skill and care. This expertise helps to explain why he had great prestige in the committee and the Senate as a whole. No other senator was so frequently mentioned in interviews with such esteem, regardless of party.

Using a similar style, Senator Francisco Bulnes, president of the Government Committee, has developed an influence that frequently overcomes partisanship. One indicator of the magnitude of respect he commands across parties is the action the committee took in response to his ruling that an important opposition amendment to the 1968 Salary Readjustment Bill was inadmissable. Bulnes was a minority president. Normally this would prohibit a president from ruling an important amendment inadmissible for fear of censure. Drawing on his expertise and experience, Bulnes felt the amendment was unconstitutional and so ruled. As might be expected, Bulnes was formally censured for partisan reasons. But some committee members knew that Bulnes had ruled correctly, according to the facts, and, when the censure came to a vote, Socialist Senator Chadwick abstained, causing a tie. A staff member gave testimony to the aura that surrounds the man: "If you want to learn how the Senate works, get an interview with 'Pancho' Bulnes, turn on the tape recorder, and just listen."

REFERENT POWER

Committee presidents like Bulnes, Alessandri, and Bossay are able to influence committee decisions not only because they are experts in the field, but also because they serve as models for other members of their committee. Each has established a reputation for being fair and honest, and they are admired across political parties because they perform their roles within the bounds set by norms of impartiality, democratic style, and tolerance. For example, Kalman H. Silvert, a well-informed student of Chilean politics, writes that Senator Bulnes is known "as a man of probity and great technical skill in performing his duties as lawmaker."[6] Members look up to this type of president and find him responsible to deal with. As long as a president continues to perform his role in this manner, members are prepared to allow him as much initiative and influence as he is willing to bear.

One former president of the Finance Committee who enjoyed a good deal of referent power was Senator Roberto Wachholtz (PR). Highly successful in private ventures, Wachholtz had been a minister of finance under President Pedro Aguirre Cerda (December 24, 1938–December 26, 1939) and minister of finance and economy in the government of Gabriel González Videla (November 3, 1946–January 10, 1947) before serving as senator from Santiago in 1959–1965. This professional expertise and practical experience carried him to the presidency of the Finance Committee. Wachholtz established a reputation

---

[6] Kalman H. Silvert, *Chile: Yesterday and Today*, p. 100.

for hard work and careful study in committee before taking sides on a bill, and other members were stimulated to work harder by his example. When he spoke, other members listened. One staff member recalled: "Wachholtz was one president who was able to get a lot done through knowledge and personality. Members seemed to work harder when he was in the chair. He knew how to keep the senators on the subject at hand, and he could compromise when it was necessary."

Another example of a president who exercises considerable influence on the Finance Committee's decisions because members admire and identify with him is Socialist Senator Aniceto Rodríguez. Unlike most of his colleagues, Rodríguez did not have a college education when he entered the Senate. But what he lacked in formal education he made up for with hard work and sound judgment. As the years progressed, Rodríguez established a reputation as a serious and responsible senator, and colleagues across political parties began to seek his opinion on key legislation.

Interview statements by an ideologically opposed senator who was also a member of the Finance Committee give testimony to Rodríguez's referent power. When answering the question, "What role ought the president of a committee play to be more effective in his work?" this senator (as well as an independent staff member) mentioned Rodríguez's style as one of a model president. Probing further, a staff member added that he had observed that committee members looked to Rodríguez not only for his opinion on a particular bill, but also to arbitrate disputes. "He has the ability to be fair, and this commands the respect of the committee members."

REWARD AND NEGATIVE POWER

Wilbur Mills, chairman of the U.S. House Ways and Means Committee, lacks many important formal prerogatives available to leaders of many organizations, but John F. Manley concludes that he fashions reward and negative power out of a series of exchanges between himself and the members, utilizing a personal style that relies on persuasion, negotiation, and bargaining.[7]

---

[7] Manley, "The House Committee on Ways and Means: 1947–1966," pp. 142–144.

Although presidents of Chilean Senate committees exercise some reward and negative power, it appears to be far less than that for a U.S. congressional committee chairman. This is so for several reasons. First of all, a president is checked by the reality that he may not have majority support in committee. Second, there is no tradition prohibiting censure, as in the U.S. Congress. Third, he is constrained by the Senate norms outlined above. Finally, he realizes that the use of negative sanctions by one president could ignite partisan reaction throughout the committee system.

Because of these factors, it is not surprising to find that fashioning this rather limited base of power requires far more skill in the management of interpersonal relations than is the case in the United States. Interviews and observation also suggest a corollary—presidents who have the most referent power also appear to enjoy the most reward and negative power, even when they are minority presidents. Put another way, identification and respect for a president may on certain occasions induce a majority of the committee to support his use of formal authority to reward or sanction a particular member, even when partisan interests are involved.

Within the broad limitations outlined above, a president has several opportunities to reward committee members. For example, he may agree to place a member's bill at the top of a committee calendar. Once the bill is before the committee, he may also cite the witnesses this member requests. Although the president of a committee normally defends a bill on the floor, he also can step aside and allow the interested senator to take the publicity and credit for passage.

Frequently, important constituents travel to Santiago to urge the consideration of a particular piece of legislation. On these occasions, a president can use his power to reward members in several ways. One option is to agree to hear the constituent's case. Another is to take the opportunity of this meeting to praise the member's judicious efforts to get the bill passed. Or, the president may help get the member off the hook by explaining to the concerned constituent that he and the majority of the committee cannot vote for the bill in its present form.

Perhaps the most important tool the president has to reward or sanction members is the authority to tolerate or to reject members' amendments to executive legislation. Tolerating these amendments and granting the other favors mentioned above give a president a line of credit he can attempt to use at a later date, either to influence member behavior or as part of an effort to counterbalance his minority status (if that is the case).

CONCLUSION

The role of president of a Chilean Senate committee appears to be somewhat less powerful than the corresponding role of chairman of a U.S. congressional committee. The great majority of the senators interviewed chose the term "important" versus the alternatives of "powerful" or "symbolic" to describe the position. Although the formal prerogatives are similar, their use is constrained by several factors: the normal lack of majority support in committee; no tradition that prohibits censure; existence of Senate norms of impartiality, democratic demeanor, and tolerance; and the realization that a president's behavior in one committee may set off a partisan reaction in other committees.

Nonetheless, some presidents are able to fashion their legitimate authority into effective power by drawing on their expertise and identification as referent leaders. This gives us one reason why senators perceive the role in the intermediate range of "important" versus "powerful" or only "symbolic." Another and perhaps more important reason implied in senators' comments is that presidents often augment the committee system's independence from national political party leadership by helping to dampen partisanship and by encouraging the interparty cooperation and compromise necessary for majority decisions.

6. Legislative and Party Leadership

MAJORITY-BUILDING is a particularly difficult task in a multiparty system where the Senate is partially elected in offyears from the president of the republic. Rarely, if ever, does a party have a majority in the Senate, not to mention the Chamber. Further, although Senate committees provide an environment for cross-party cooperation, they also seem to enjoy an intermediate level of independence from most national party policy bodies. Hence there is a need for Senate mechanisms that coordinate and control the majority-building process across parties and guide intraparty legislation in committees and on the floor.

The Senate legislative leadership structure consists of the president of the Senate, political party floor leaders, interparty conferences, and party caucuses. Senators' expectations for the role of president of the

Senate and past incumbents' behavior normally encourage interparty cooperation and compromise. In addition, recruitment to the position of floor leader for all political parties emphasizes norms of cooperation and work more than norms of partisanship. Finally, weekly Senate party caucuses provide an arena for overall policy coordination and control, as does the government party (PDC) tri-party arrangement to enhance policy coordination and development between congressional caucuses, the national party leadership, and the executive branch.

PRESIDENT OF THE SENATE

At the beginning of each legislative period, a president and vice-president (to serve in the president's absence) are elected to preside over the Senate (together called the Mesa Directiva).[1] Since no single party ordinarily has a majority, the Mesa is generally elected by a coalition of several parties that may not follow strict ideological lines, as was the case when Salvador Allende (PS) was elected by the Communist, Socialist, and Radical parties in 1966. Indeed, the president and vice-president may be members of opposing parties as, for example, when Fernando Alessandri (PL) and Salvador Allende (PS) served together from 1951 to 1955.

As a rule, long tenure suggests that the Mesa has the confidence of the majority bloc of senators. The Mesa (individually or jointly) may be censured by any senator, but this is more symbolic than real as long as the majority that elected them stays intact.

The Senate Rules give the president (and in his absence, the vice-president) a number of formal prerogatives. He may cite special sessions, order floor debates, recognize senators, interpret the Senate Rules, declare whether an amendment is constitutional or inadmissible, act in the name of the Senate when it is in recess, preside over meetings with party floor leaders, conduct routine Senate correspondence, and guard the liberty and respect of the Senate as an institution.[2]

In fact, Senate expectations govern how this formal authority should be exercised. Wahlke, Eulau, Buchanan, and Ferguson note that the

---

[1] Víctor Engber Álvarez, *Los presidentes de las cámaras*, pp. 72–75.
[2] "Reglamento del senado," *Manual del senado*, pp. 119–122.

British Parliament arranged many years ago to elevate the speaker above the party struggle once he had been elected and to give him authority to referee the game. He is neutralized from party politics.[3] On the other hand, the U.S. Congress and U.S. state legislatures do not follow this example. Although these speakers are expected to be fair and impartial, they are simultaneously majority party leaders.[4]

Interviews show that the president of the Chilean Senate more closely resembles the British model.[5] When senators and staff were asked, "As you see it, what role ought the President play in order to be more effective in his job?" 95 percent of the senators and 93 percent of the staff responding (thirty-eight and thirteen, respectively) felt he should be impartial and detached from partisan politics while presiding. Most revealing are statements by two past presidents of the Senate, one a member of a party of the Right, and the other from the Left:

> The president should not participate in debates, and must guarantee equal rights to all parties. He can also help to keep the parties apart. Sometimes, I wanted to participate in debates. But then I said to myself, a statement now will only encourage more comments, so I just kept quiet. And that's why I got elected with the 100 percent support of all parties.

> The president should defend the Senate itself. On one occasion, a deputy of my own party spoke out against the Senate as being obstructionist. Well, I protested that statement publicly.

Acceptance speeches of newly elected presidents give testimony to the existence of Senate norms that prescribe his expected behavior. It is a ritual in the Senate for a new president to pay tribute to these norms

[3] John C. Wahlke *et al.*, *The Legislative System: Explorations in Legislative Behavior*, p. 175.

[4] Kenneth R. Mackenzie, *The English Parliament*, ch. 8, cited in Wahlke *et al.*, *The Legislative System*, p. 176.

[5] Engber Álvarez, *Los presidentes de las cámaras*, p. 102. It is probably more accurate to compare the president of the Senate with presiding officers in legislatures of Commonwealth and continental European countries. Although the president is expected to preside impartially and to be detached from parties as in Britain, he does not continue in office if a congressional election alters the majority bloc. Nor are attempts made to ensure that he is not opposed in his constituency at re-election. Similiarly, he need not pledge never to return to party politics at some future date.

and promise to observe them. Witness excerpts from three speeches covering the period from 1933 to 1969:

> I accept this honor with the understanding that I have been elected as a member of a nonpartisan *Mesa* . . . and that this is in harmony with the Constitution. (Alberto Cabero Díaz, PR, 1933)[6]
>
> I will be a faithful guardian of the Senate Rules that protect the rights of the Senate and all of its members. . . . Senators, I will protect the prestige of this high body. This is my most important duty. To protect its prestige is to protect the democratic regime, public liberty, and the stability of the law. (Fernando Alessandri, PL, 1953)[7]
>
> Notwithstanding the political position of those who elected us, we will not have a Senate habitually opposed [to the Government] . . . I can say that all of the Senators will receive equal and just treatment which has been the constant norm of the Chilean Parliament. (Salvador Allende, PS, 1966)[8]

As a rule, the president of the Senate faithfully keeps his promise, and it is customary to acknowledge this fact *across parties* at the end of his term.

> Fernando Alessandri, as president of the Senate for an extended period, has directed debates and represented the Senate with tact, consideration, and patriotism that deserves the unanimous recognition of the citizenry of the country. (applause) (Perez de Arche, National Ibáñez Movement, 1958)[9]

This prescribed style places the president of the Senate in a position to dampen partisan conflicts on the floor, to referee disputes, and to act as a catalyst for interparty cooperation and compromise. Typical comments were: "He should keep the parties apart," "encourage private contacts between the parties," and "orient meetings between

---

[6] *Diario de sesiones del senado, legislatura ordinaria*, sesión 1a, May 23, 1933, p. 63.

[7] *Diario de sesiones del senado, legislatura ordinaria*, sesión 1a, May 26, 1953, pp. 21–22.

[8] *Diario de sesiones del senado, legislatura extraordinaria*, sesión 43a, December 27, 1966, pp. 2594–2595.

[9] *Diario de sesiones del senado, legislatura extraordinaria*, sesión 6a, April 8, 1958, p. 203.

floor leaders." More specifically, the president may ask for a short recess if the debate takes on the color of heated partisan exchanges. Or he can call to a particular senator's attention that the Senate Rules require indirect address by way of the chair, use of the term "Honorable" when referring to a colleague, and avoidance of personal defamatory attacks. He may also rule unconstitutional or inadmissible a particular article or amendment inspired by partisan in-fighting.

Perhaps his greatest opportunity to encourage cross-party compromise is in the meetings with political party floor leaders. Prior to Senate sessions and on other special occasions, floor leaders meet in the office of the president to arrange the calendar and timing of bills and to reach agreements on other matters such as the position of the Senate on an urgency request from the executive. The manner in which the president conducts these sessions determines in large measure whether the level of partisanship rises or falls. One senator said, "The personal style of the president has a big impact on how things move along."

Traditionally, the president of the Senate has been a force for non-partisanship, conciliation, and the search for the national interest. He is expected to represent what the Senate as an institution stands for. The majority of the members interviewed understand this to mean "maintaining a civic equilibrium." The Chamber is expected to represent every popular current of opinion and interest group demand. But senators like to think that they should function above all this. They point out that one of the reasons for adopting a partial election system for the Senate was an attempt to insulate the body from partisan demands. The majority (90%, or twenty-six of the twenty-nine senators responding) see themselves first as representatives of the nation before political parties and constituencies, and several advocate revising the Constitution to provide for national rather than regional election. The Senate, they believe, should revise and moderate the Chamber's bills— whether that signifies movements to the Left or the Right. The president, by the force of his personality and example, can reinforce this national role orientation.

But not every president is suited by temperament, desire, or past political experience to play this role. A case in point is Salvador Allende. Elected by a bloc of parties who frequently oppose government

(PDC) programs, Allende pledged to chair the Senate in an impartial manner. As far as the Senate Rules are concerned, he has met expectations. One ideologically opposed National senator pointed out that even he had to admit that Allende interpreted the Senate Rules fairly and objectively.

But, looking at role behavior as a whole, one discovers that the norms that define this role are not always observed. For example, the president of the Senate is expected to preside at the joint session of Congress every year when the president of the Republic gives his annual message (May 21). Allende refused to do so for partisan reasons in 1968. As president of the Senate, he is expected to show institutional patriotism inside and outside the body. This norm presumes a belief in democratic institutions and the role of the Senate in particular. Yet in 1968 Allende was president of an organization called OLAS, which advocated the violent overthrow of democratic institutions. One highly respected former Senate president said: "Allende has taken the position that he doesn't have to give up his role as a political militant just because he is president of the Senate. In fact, it's impossible to fulfill both roles, in my opinion." A senator from another party added: "Allende's connections with OLAS and his recent treatment of Bolivian revolutionaries is not correct. It hurts the prestige of the Senate."

Reaction to Allende's violation of traditional role behavior indicates the degree to which actions of the president influence the level of partisanship in the body. A typical comment, for example, was, "Allende is a combatant; he is trying to take advantage of the visibility of this position to push himself." Another senator added: "There is a lot more partisanship under Allende than there should be. For example, he told Bulnes to hurry up when he was debating the Salary Readjustment Bill. But when Teitelboim spoke, he didn't. Why? Because they are political friends."

FLOOR LEADERS AND INTRAPARTY CONFERENCES

As noted above, the president of the Senate regularly meets before sessions, and on other important matters, with floor leaders (numbering two for each party or group of three or more independent senators). The development of floor leadership positions is a twentieth-century phenomenon in the Chilean Senate. Beginning informally at first in the 1920's and 1930's, the positions gained official recognition in the Senate Rules of 1953.[10] As the level of party discipline increased, the positions gained more authority.

Interviews indicate that floor leaders today function like the majority and minority leaders and whips in the U.S. Senate and enjoy comparable influence within their respective parties. When senators were asked, "Is a floor leader a powerful position, or only symbolic?" 86 percent of the senators responding (thirty-six) perceived the role as important, very important, or powerful. When political party is controlled, we find that four of the five senators who did not regard the position as important were members of the National party. This probably reflects the fact that these senators tend to exercise more influence on the national party leadership's policy stand than vice versa, and because Senator Bulnes appears to be the real caucus leader, although he is not formally a floor leader.

First of all, floor leaders act as the line of communication to and from the national party leadership outside the Senate. It seems logical, since floor leaders in the Senate are frequently national party leaders as well—for example, Senators Rodríquez (PS), Palma (PDC), and Teitelboim (PC). This involves transmitting Senate party caucus views to the national party and vice versa. When party orders are issued, it is the job of the floor leaders to make sure each senator is aware of them and to grant any exceptions that members may ask for before the bill reaches the floor. Similarly, if the Senate caucus is unanimously opposed to a national party stand, the floor leaders are expected to argue for a change.

Second, floor leaders manage national party and caucus affairs inside the Senate. This includes leading weekly party caucus meetings and arbitrating disputes over assignments to committees. They also insure that the regular member of a committee is replaced if he must be absent for one reason or another. As in the U.S. Congress, a pair system exists. Floor leaders formally approve each of these agreements

---

[10] Gilberto Moreno G., *Los comités parlamentarios*, pp. 70–73.

in order to be sure that votes are available when necessary. On many key bills, each party has an allocated period of time to speak on the floor. Floor leaders dictate who should speak for the party, and for approximately how long. It is also their task to make sure that an adequate number of members are on the floor and voting when required, and in certain instances they have the authority to order senators to vote jointly even when national party orders have not been issued. They also are responsible for watching out for other party interests on the floor. Typical tasks are requesting that a bill be moved from one floor calendar to another, asking that a document be entered in the transcript of Senate sessions or that debates be published in volume for public distribution, and moving to censure the Mesa of the Senate.

Third, floor leaders represent their party in joint meetings with other party leaders, which are chaired by the president of the Senate. Each party group's votes are weighed according to the number of senators they represent. Decisions by this group can markedly speed up or slow down the work of the Senate. For example, party leaders may jointly vote to: call special sessions (majority), bypass committee review of a bill (two-thirds), rearrange the floor calendar (two-thirds), reserve a place for a bill on the calendar of the next regular session (majority), refuse to prolong debates on a bill for another day (two-thirds), make floor votes roll-call and public (unanimous), extend the day's session (unanimous), and allow committees to meet at the same hours as the session (unanimous).[11]

Normally the government party or coalition does not have a majority of the seats in the Senate and therefore lacks control over floor leaders' decisions. If the main or sole objective of the non-government parties was to obstruct legislation initiated by the administration, these policy and procedural meetings would be one key means for doing so. It is significant that these meetings result in cross-party cooperation and compromise, not in impasse.

First of all, minor bills and routine procedural decisions are passed by unanimous consent. These decisions are binding on all Senate members on the floor. On major policy matters, leaders appear to concen-

[11] "Reglamento del Senado," in *Manual del senado*, pp. 118–119.

trate on a search for avenues of agreement and compromise that avoid sterile confrontations on the floor. For example, take the 1968 Education Reform Bill. President Frei and Education Minister Pacheco were eager to see early passage, especially in the face of recent student and faculty pleas for reform. Frei requested an urgency classification in the Senate. Under pressure to dispatch the bill, Christian-Democrat floor leaders sought to sound out opposition leaders, who, it was clear, wanted more time to study it in committee than an urgency classification would provide. Meeting together, floor leaders reached a compromise solution. In return for government retirement of the urgency request, the floor leaders agreed to set a time limit of sixty days for study of the bill in committee (twice that of an urgency classification). As an added face-saving measure that facilitated this agreement, floor leaders representing the Christian-Democrat, Radical, Communist, and Socialist parties issued a public statement, which read in part: "This compromise does not signify that the floor leaders support the bill as it was sent by the Chamber to the Senate . . . it is simply an acceptance of a time limit to study legislation adequately, responsibly, and efficiently."[12]

Four variables appear to facilitate compromise among floor leaders. First of all, although certain differences do exist between political parties, they all appear to share an overriding consensus on regime support.[13] This consensus discourages individual partisanship, thereby reducing ideological rigidity and unrealistic conflict.[14] As a result, Chilean scholar Osvaldo Sunkel notes, all parties including the far Left (Communist and Socialist parties) concentrate on legislative measures to secure short-run social benefits.[15]

[12] *Declaración de los comités comunista, demócrata cristiano, radical y socialista del senado en relación con el estudio del proyecto que legisla sobre las universidades*, n.d.

[13] K. H. Silvert, "The Prospects of Chilean Democracy: Some Propositions on Chile," *Latin American Politics: 24 Studies of the Contemporary Scene*, ed. Robert D. Tomasek, p. 396.

[14] For a discussion of this process, see Lewis A. Coser, *The Functions of Social Conflict*, pp. 34–35, 58–59, 77–80.

[15] Osvaldo Sunkel, "Change and Frustration in Chile," in *Obstacles to Change in Latin America*, ed. Claudio Veliz, p. 132.

Achievement of these short-run objectives through compromise is facilitated by two other variables. As in Senate committees, floor leader meetings are closed, private, and off the record unless a press release is mutually agreed to. The secretary of the Senate keeps a record of the proceedings (*actas*), but they are not released to the public. This environment facilitates a free give and take across parties that leads to overall agreements. Furthermore, the president of the Senate normally aids this process. As presiding officer, he can insure that every party leader has an equal opportunity to express his views. Reminding leaders of their commitment to the national interest and controlling the partisanship of the discussion, he steers the leaders toward a common ground on policy and procedural matters.

The fourth and probably most significant variable influencing floor leaders' behavior is that the great majority of senators *across parties* expect them to exhibit a pragmatic style. Senators were asked, "What role ought a floor leader play in order to be more effective in his job?" Although 65 percent (twenty-two) of the senators responding (thirty-four) emphasized a partisan norm (i.e., he should seek to represent the majority sentiment within his party), the *largest majority* indicated a programmatic orientation by emphasizing norms of cooperation and work. Seventy-seven percent (twenty-six) expected their floor leaders to bargain across parties, and 62 percent (twenty-one) expected them to facilitate the Senate work. A typical comment was, "He should have many years of political experience, good judgment, and solid relations with other parties."

Being the minority government party, the Christian-Democrats are particularly conscious of the need for a skilled floor leader to help strike bargains between parties that aid passage of their own programs. One Christian-Democrat senator noted: "He has to have personal agility. I've seen where ———— got a lot that officially he shouldn't have—just out of personal respect." An opposition senator noted that the Christian-Democrats usually made sure that each floor leader represented a wing of the party. This move not only gained support for their decisions within the party, but also enabled one to deal with parties of the Left (e.g., via Senator Rafael Gumucio) and the other with the Right (e.g., Senator Ignacio Palma).

Through exchange relationships, each party seeks to obtain some of their objectives. For example, the National party supported the Christian-Democrats' 1966 Chileanization Copper Bill in exchange for a slowdown in the agrarian reform program. The Communist party aided passage of the 1968 Salary Readjustment Bill after the Christian-Democrats agreed to delete a no-strike provision in the bill. Arranging these bargains takes great personal skill and ability. Hence, each party seeks to select a floor leader who not only speaks in the name of his own party, but also has a personal style capable of obtaining the greatest possible advantages from other parties. Said one government senator, "He has to have a good personal *trato* [style], not be a constant agitator [*peleador*]"; another agreed, "We can't have a leader who is always fighting and creating resentment." A third senator, reviewing the skills required and recognizing that he did not have them, candidly blurted out, "I've never been a floor leader because I'm not a very conciliatory type."

Staff members' comments give us further insight into the skills required of an effective floor leader. "He should be skillful and not upset people [*hábil—no pica la gente*]. You need the intelligence to be able to conceal what is in your interest. Often, the senators who hardly ever speak on the floor are the best party leaders, because they don't put anyone on the spot publicly." A second, who had traveled to the United States and visited the Senate, made this comparison: "The best way to describe them is they are nuts-and-bolts bargainers, like your President Johnson. This is what we call a *pasillero*. That's a senator you often see arm in arm with another while they walk down the corridors of the Senate thrashing out some kind of deal."

PARTY CAUCUSES (OR CONFERENCES)

The main intraparty center for coordinating Senate party policy is the party caucus or conference. Party caucuses seldom meet in the U.S. Congress, and when they do they have little if any authority over members.[16] Similarly, most U.S. state legislatures seldom have caucuses that meet regularly. Chile contrasts sharply in this regard. Since there

[16] Malcolm E. Jewell and Samuel C. Patterson, *The Legislative Process in the United States*, pp. 184–190.

are only forty-five members in the Senate divided into several smaller party groups, the caucus becomes an effective device for discussing party policy.

At the beginning of each legislative period, senators for each of the respective parties meet first to elect floor leaders and allocate committee seats (except the Communist party, which makes recommendations to the national party). The floor leaders are elected first, and they then preside over the allocation of committee seats and begin the process of coordinating party policy.

Caucuses usually meet every Tuesday for a long business luncheon before the first Senate session of the week. Sessions are closed and informal. Most of the discussion involves bills already on the Senate calendar. But other matters may be raised. For example, the floor leader may ask for a discussion on a conflict between the national party leadership and the Senate caucus—especially when the senators are unanimously opposed to a party policy. Or the floor may be opened to review what the caucus position should be in the next interparty conference on an urgency request from the president.

The floor leaders normally begin with the most important legislation on the agenda. In some instances, national party orders have been issued, and the floor leaders simply explain the position to be taken on the floor and answer any questions that arise. But party orders do not accompany most legislation, and so open discussion ensues in the caucus. Here the merits of the bill and certain articles will be reviewed. In these instances, floor leaders are frequently able to exercise important influence on the caucus position either because they are the effective leaders of the caucus or because of their overlapping role as president or member of a top Senate committee. Knowledge gained through committee study enables them to explain the bill and its articles and to warn about details to watch out for. This sways votes.

The Christian-Democrat party attempts to maintain good policy communication and coordination between Chamber and Senate caucuses, the executive council of the national party, and President Frei's ministries by a triparty arrangement. For example, when the education minister has developed legislation reforming the Chilean education system, he requests a joint meeting with the technical and policy officials of the national party and congressional representatives from each chamber (usually floor leaders). The proposal is discussed and usually substantially modified before submission to Congress. As part of this process, a Senate floor leader may bring the issue up in caucus, explain the key aspects of the bill, and solicit opinions. Trial testings among opposition senators may also be made. This feedback will be channeled to the minister, and perhaps one or more joint meetings held before agreement is reached. Evidently, senators have ample opportunity to influence government policy through this linkage. Furthermore, this process helps to insure caucus support for the bill once it reaches the Senate.

But caucuses are not always effective in achieving a united stand on an issue and may even create sharper divisions within the Senate party. Floor leaders are expected, in effect, to wear two hats—that of a national party spokesman and that of Senate party leader. At times, the roles may conflict. For example, an issue arose once during the present administration (1966) quite similar to the conflict between former President Eisenhower and Senator Knowland. Senator Gumucio (PDC) was acting as the party floor leader and was expected to support administration policy in the caucus as well as on the Senate floor. Gumucio disagreed with government policy and publicly opposed the stand. Afterward, Gumucio resigned as floor leader. One senator reported, "Gumucio felt he couldn't remain as floor leader because he didn't agree with government policy. The role calls for someone who can agree to be effective."

CONCLUSION

Two major problems face a government party in the Chilean Senate: (1) the difficulty of building a working majority in a multiparty environment, and (2) a committee system that has an intermediate level of autonomy, apart from party leadership. Three mechanisms within the legislative leadership structure help to overcome these obstacles. First is the role of president of the Senate. Senators expect the president to act inside and outside the Senate in an impartial and nonpartisan manner. Traditionally, presidents have met these expectations, thereby serving as a force to dampen partisan conflicts on the floor, to referee disputes, and to encourage interparty cooperation and compromise in joint conferences.

The second mechanism is interparty conferences chaired by the president of the Senate, which normally lead to majority agreement on many important policy and procedural matters. Four variables explain this fact: (1) there appears to be an overriding consensus on regime support; (2) interparty conferences are closed and off the record; (3) the president of the Senate steers discussions so as to reduce partisanship; (4) senator expectations defining the role of floor leader emphasize cooperation and work over partisanship.

The third mechanism is the caucus, which serves as a center for intraparty coordination and control. The government party (PDC) attempts through a triparty arrangement to insure that policy communication between the national party, executive ministries, and congressional caucuses functions adequately to reach agreements as well as to sound out opposition leaders on major legislation. This process helps aid passage of government bills once they reach the Senate. These three mechanisms of the leadership structure, combined with a committee environment that discourages partisanship, and formal and informal rules of the game that govern Senate behavior provide an adequate institutional infrastructure for the interparty cooperation and decision-making necessary for political and economic development.

7. Formal and Informal Rules

JEWELL AND PATTERSON have argued that if we "are to begin more adequately to understand and explain the legislative policy-making process, we must learn about the context, the setting, in which policy is or is not made."[1] This requires an understanding of both the formal and informal rules of the game that define how legislators are expected to behave.[2]

NOTE: Portions of this chapter originally appeared in *Comparative Legislative Systems*, ed. M. Donald Hancock and Herbert Hirsch (Glencoe, Ill.: The Free Press, 1971) and are used here in revised form with the permission of the publisher.

[1] Malcolm E. Jewell and Samuel C. Patterson, *The Legislative Process in the United States*, p. 361.

[2] Formal rules have long been a subject of study for political scientists. Inability to understand legislative behavior by relying only on the formal structure and rules has led scholars to examine informal norms or rules as well. Examples of more

Organization theorists have at times characterized these written and unwritten rules as an organizational culture. Selznick, for example, states: "In each organization, then, there grow certain patterns of conduct and belief. These are considered 'right' for the organization in the general consensus."[3] Pfiffner and Sherwood continue that it is within this context that all members are expected to operate. "The alternative ways in which an individual will be permitted to behave in any particular organization will be sharply conditioned by its institutional character."[4]

As we examined the committee and party leadership structure of the Chilean Senate in earlier chapters, we noted several norms that define member and leadership roles and set minimum standards of expected behavior. Frequently these norms lessen partisanship and encourage compromise, which in turn enables legislative decisions to be made. At this point, it is necessary to describe more fully the formal and informal Senate norms of behavior that hold the decision-making structure together. The formal rules can be divided into four main groups, rules concerning (1) committees, (2) sessions and calendars, (3) control of debate, and (4) voting. The informal rules of behavior fall into the following categories: those which decrease conflict and those which encourage performance of work and specialization. Sanctions that ensure observance of these rules are also explained. Interview comments are supported by objective data wherever possible.

FORMAL RULES

Every legislature is said to develop within a context of normative standards of proper conduct. Some legislative norms are so highly authoritative, formalized, and legitimate as to be codified into written rules of behavior. The Chilean Senate is guided by such a body of

---

recent studies are Allan Kornberg, "The Rules of the Game in the Canadian House of Commons," *Journal of Politics* 26, no. 2 (1964): 358–380; John Wahlke *et al.*, *The Legislative System: Explorations in Legislative Behavior*; Donald R. Matthews, *U.S. Senators and Their World*, ch. 5; and Nathan C. Leites, *On the Game of Politics in France*.

[3] Peter Selznick, *Leadership in Administration*, p. 251.

[4] John M. Pfiffner and Frank P. Sherwood, *Administrative Organization*, p. 250.

formal rules, by past precedents, and by the Constitution—all of which are bound together in the Senate Manual numbering 755 pages.[5] The Senate Rules (65 pages) govern most day-to-day operations of the Senate. Like the U.S. Senate, the Chilean Senate is a continuing body in that only part of its membership is elected or re-elected prior to the opening of each Congress. Similarly, the Senate Rules are not formally re-adopted, although minor modifications may be made.[6] The secretary of the Senate acts as official parliamentarian. Part of his responsibility is to be thoroughly familiar with the Rules and past precedents and to help the president of the Senate and other members to interpret them accordingly.

Committees

According to Article 45 of the Constitution, bills may be introduced by the president of the republic or by not more than five senators or ten deputies, except in areas specifically reserved to the president (see chapter 1).[7] Article 38 of the Senate Rules requires that all such bills (before both general and specific discussion) and presidential vetoes of bills approved by Congress must go to committees for review.[8] Committees may be bypassed by a unanimous floor vote or by two-thirds agreement of party floor leaders, but this is seldom moved or met if so.

Bills are assigned to each respective committee by subject matter content. The Rules specifically prescribe that all bills that signify expenditures not contained in the annual budget or that establish new taxes must be assigned to the Finance Committee. Furthermore, they require that a joint committee on the budget be set up each year to approve the budget, consisting of eleven senators (five of whom must be members of Finance) and eleven deputies. Rules also allow two committees to meet jointly to study a particular bill, and specify which president should preside for each possible combination. Generally, committees session separately unless a bill assigned to one committee by subject

---

[5] *Manual del senado.*
[6] Iván Auger Labarca, *La potestad reglamentaria de las asambleas legislativas.*
[7] "Constitución política in la república de Chile," in *Manual del senado,* p. 31.
[8] "Reglamento del senado," in *Manual del Senado,* pp. 125–126.

matter must also pass Finance because it signifies new expenses or taxes.

Article 36 of the Rules gives the president of each committee the authority to call sessions as he sees fit. A committee member or one party leader may also ask for sessions, but this seems to be rarely done through these formal channels. Article 40 gives each committee the authority to ask for information and to cite experts or witnesses it deems necessary to report on a bill; this prerogative is strengthened by Article 5 of Law 13.608, which requires administration officials to meet these requests (see chapter 1).

On paper, the urgency powers of the president of the republic, which limit the period available to dispatch a bill, appear to weaken severely the power of Senate committees to study, modify, or delay executive legislation. But, as we saw earlier, the president is often forced to retire this classification, thereby giving committees adequate time to study a bill. For example, Rules allow party floor leaders to set time limits when committees must report out a bill. Normally, they use this authority to lengthen the time committees have to study a bill rather than shorten it. For example, the urgency classification of the 1968 Education Reform Bill was retired by the president in exchange for a compromise solution that increased the length of time the committees of Education and Finance had to study the bill. Furthermore, floor leaders customarily let committees decide when (if ever) they will dispatch much important and most middle- and lower-range legislation.

Sessions and Calendars

There are three types of legislative sessions: ordinary, extraordinary, and special. Ordinary sessions run from May 21 to September 18 each year and normally include two sessions (Tuesday and Wednesday) for three hours each from 4 P.M. to 7 P.M.[9] In recent years, extraordinary or special sessions have been called immediately after the close of regular sessions that have come to last until the opening of the next regular session, thereby keeping the Senate in session virtually the year round. Extraordinary sessions may be called by either the president of the

---

[9] Our field observation indicates that the Senate sessions more frequently run for longer hours when key matters must be dispatched.

republic or the Senate, although the president generally has done so. When the executive calls such a session, the senate must limit itself to dealing exclusively with matters included in the convocation. If the Senate calls the session, it is free to deal with whatever it chooses.

Ordinary sessions (which we will be concerned with here) are divided into two periods: (1) minutes, reports, easy dispatch, order of the day, and voting; (2) incidental matters. As in the United States, the Senate handles many routine bills of a noncontroversial nature. The method used to dispatch these bills rapidly is to set aside thirty minutes during the first part of the session, which is known as *easy dispatch* and may be extended for a longer period of time by a unanimous floor vote. Similar to the consent calendar in the U.S. House of Representatives, routine bills of minor importance are included and passed by voice vote. The president of the Senate makes up the calendar and the order of the bills contained. But any party floor leader may ask that a bill be removed, in which case it may not be returned without his approval. Every Tuesday the president of the Senate announces the calendar that will be voted on the following week.

Easy dispatch is followed by the order-of-the-day calendar, which lasts a minimum of one hour and a half. It may be extended for an additional hour by a two-thirds vote of the senators present or for a longer period by a unanimous vote. All bills not placed on the calendar of easy dispatch appear here, including such important business as accusations against a minister. Rules specify how the calendar must be ordered. First priority goes to charges of conflict of interest against a senator, accusations against ministers and other officials, national budget, bills with an urgency classification, and other preferential matters. This business is followed by bills that have already been to the floor for general discussion and are now in one of the more advanced stages (e.g., specific discussion, consideration of Chamber's modification of Senate version, after presidential veto).

The balance of the calendar is arranged by the president of the Senate after meeting with the various party floor leaders. This calendar arrangement is usually followed. But recent developments may require alterations, and Senate Rules accordingly provide some flexibility. For example, floor leaders representing two-thirds of the Senate may alter the calendar of the same session, and a unanimous floor vote is sufficient to place on the floor business that is not on the calendar. Similarly, floor leaders representing a majority of the Senate may move to give preference in the next session to a bill already on the calendar.

Because the executive has the power to declare legislation urgent, which gives it priority on the calendar, it is not surprising that these bills dominate the Senate's time. But, as noted earlier, floor leaders who represent the majority of the Senate can force the executive to retire his urgency classification, to modify the bills, to give the Senate more time, or at least to tolerate several amendments. Thus, directly and indirectly, floor leaders exercise important control over the calendar despite the executive's urgency powers.

Incidental Matters

Following floor votes on the calendar bills, the Senate begins the second period of its sessions known as the *hora de incidentes* (incidental hour). At this time senators can bring up or debate any matter, except actual bills, that they judge to be in the public interest or compatible with their public responsibilities. This period not only performs a cathartic function but also encourages the various political parties to look on the Senate as one arena where they will have an opportunity to present their views in proportion to their strength in the Senate. Specifically, the Rules give each party thirty minutes for its first four senators and five minutes more for each senator over four. Independents and parties who have less than four senators divide thirty minutes among them. The order in which each party will speak is determined by mutual agreement of floor leaders, or, barring this, by order of the number of seats each party has in the Senate. One party may, if it wishes, allot some of its time to another party. Internally, party caucuses agree with their floor leader as to who will be allowed to speak, and this is communicated to the other party floor leaders during the interparty conference preceding each session.

Rules allow these sessions to be printed in volume for public distribution after unanimous floor approval. It is a Senate norm to vote reciprocally for each senator's request, which is rarely denied except as a social sanction for unacceptable behavior. These speeches are then distributed by each senator when he visits his district to show how hard he is working for its interests.

Control over Debate
ORDER AND DECORUM

Two groups of procedural rules govern debate: those which help provide order and decorum and those which expedite business. Floor debates before a ready public press and full public galleries provide senators with the opportunity of increasing their personal prestige, aiding an upcoming campaign, and centering attention on particular issues. In the zeal to achieve these ends, it would be quite easy for debates to become heated and to degenerate into personal attacks, thereby decreasing the likelihood of interparty agreements on or off the floor. It is significant then that Senate debates are conducted on a high plane, and that one frequently sees opposing senators on the floor later arm in arm in the hallways or amicably taking tea (once) together in the Senate dining room. One is struck by the great difference between the Chamber and the Senate debates in this regard. If the Chamber debates are characterized by noise and personal attacks, the Senate's are noted for their relatively calm, amicable deliberations. Part of the difference may be accounted for by the smaller size of the Senate, and part by the Senate's unwritten norms, which we will discuss shortly. But a third variable is the Senate Rules governing debates.

The president of the Senate is responsible for maintaining order and decorum in the Senate. Rules require that each senator solicit permission from the president in order to speak. Normally, he is expected to give the floor in the order asked. But Rules allow him the discretion of altering the order to ensure that each political party or representing senator has an equal opportunity to defend his views. Judicious use of this prerogative conditions senators to listen calmly while others speak, because they know they can expect their turn. Rules also require senators to address each other as "Honorable" and to refrain from personal attacks. Article 97 provides a slandered senator preferential use of the floor for ten minutes to respond to an injurious speech, and Article 120 allows the president to call the offending senator to order or even to deprive him of his right to participate in debates, if necessary.

Awareness that these sanctions can be applied, in addition to informal Senate norms, keeps debates within acceptable bounds. But on occasion, and especially before elections, the partisan pitch of debates tends to rise. The president of the Senate may then give senators an opportunity to regain their composure and return debates to normal. For example, he may suspend sessions temporarily while senators cool off or have tea. This enables disagreeing senators to settle their differences in private or, at the very least, to regain some control over their emotions.

EXPEDITION OF BUSINESS

Rules that expedite business appear to be somewhat stricter than in the U.S. Senate. The first group deals with urgency legislation. Despite all the hurdles the Senate raises (see chapter 1), some executive bills are classified urgent and are passed through the Senate rather rapidly (along with Senate amendments). Once a bill has such a classification, and if it is not withdrawn by the president of the republic before it reaches the floor, a time limit is specified to report the bill out of committee, to debate, and to vote on it on the floor. Debate is closed at the end of the time period and voting begun. Of course, the Senate can and often does vote to reject the bill within the required time limit.[10]

The second group governs closure, which may be obtained by a 60 percent vote of those present, compared to 66 percent in the U.S. Senate. For all nonurgency bills, closure may be moved after three sessions of debate during the general discussion. If rejected, the motion may be raised again after two more sessions of debate. During the specific article-by-article discussion, closure may be moved on a particular article or group of articles after one session of debate. If rejected, a move may be renewed the following session. On succeeding stages of the bill, closure is possible after only two opposing discussions. Although difficult, it is possible to reopen debate on particular articles if two-thirds of the senators agree.

When a bill is not urgent or closure has not been moved, a third group of rules limits debate. One is the right to move previous ques-

[10] Article 138 of the Senate Rules also limits to two the number of urgency bills that may be considered simultaneously in committee or on the floor.

tion, a motion that is nondebatable and calls for an immediate vote on a pending bill. Rules also disallow questions to be raised that are not pertinent to the issue at hand, although observation suggests that this is applied somewhat sparingly. Rules further limit each senator's speeches to no more than two on the same matter for the general and specific discussions of a bill.

Voting

If a bill is approved after a general discussion, amendments may be made that go with the bill to committee for a second report prior to an article-by-article discussion. The president of the Senate and the committee presidents have the authority to rule inadmissible amendments that are not germane to the bill's content, that are not financed, or that are considered to be unconstitutional. In practice, amendments not pertinent to the subject matter of the bill are frequently allowed, as in the U.S. Senate. Committees do eliminate some of them, but the majority go to the floor for specific discussion and vote. A motion to recommit a bill to committee or to table usually effectively kills it.

Formally, the president of the Senate is responsible for arranging the order of floor votes on a bill. In fact, he, together with floor leaders, decides the exact procedure. For example, the 1968 Salary Readjustment Bill was divided into articles where agreement was unanimous and passed by voice vote. The remaining articles were debated and voted on one by one.

A system of pairing is also used in the Chilean Senate. Most pairing must be formally approved by the respective party leaders and recorded with the secretary of the Senate, although occasionally some short-term agreements in fact are not. Pairs may be for short- or long-term periods or even only for specific bills. Voting may be public or secret, by voice or roll. As in most legislatures, the most common method used is the voice vote. A review of the Senate debates, however, indicates that votes after the general discussion of many important bills (e.g., 1966 Chileanization Copper Bill) are recorded by individual. Unfortunately, article-by-article and amendment votes at the specific stage are not published except in aggregate form. But personal observation of floor voting on the 1968 Salary Readjustment Bill showed that the secretary of the Senate does record votes by individual as the roll is called, and the results may be obtainable informally.

The Senate Rules have tried to avoid conflict-of-interest charges by specifying that a senator should not vote on a bill that involves his private activities. Prior to roll-call votes, senators are given five minutes each to explain their stand if they want to. Party leaders use such procedural devices as pairs and abstention to allow party members to meet pressure-group or constituency commitments without directly voting contrary to other party members.

These formal rules, together with informal norms, constitute the primary guideposts to accepted behavior that enables the Senate to make decisions without tearing itself apart.

INFORMAL RULES OF THE GAME

Traditionally, political parties in Chile have formed temporary blocs or coalitions large enough to ensure a majority vote on legislation. During the legislative period under study (1965–1969), the government party (PDC) has attempted to govern by relying on other parties for support on an issue-by-issue basis rather than by resorting to a formal coalition. What attracts attention is that opposing political parties have cooperated with the Christian-Democrat party in the Senate to pass major legislation. For example, the government passed the 1966 Chileanization Copper Bill with the support of the National and Radical parties, while the 1966 Agrarian Reform Bill passed with the Communist and Radical parties' votes. The 1968 Salary Readjustment Bill left the Senate with the support of *both* the National and Communist parties—polar opposites ideologically.

Evidently, ideologically opposed political parties are capable of controlling partisan differences sufficiently to act on issues on which the members basically agree.[11] This capacity may in turn be dependent on certain rules of the game that set the approximate limits of expected behavior required to obtain the respect and cooperation of opposing parties' members. If this is so, tapping senators' and staff's perceptions

---

[11] See Charles W. Anderson's comments on policy consensus in Chile in *Politics and Economic Change in Latin America: The Governing of Restless Nations*, p. 197.

as to the existence of such unwritten rules of behavior and their functions may give us empirical proof that this description is correct.

Senators and staff were asked, "Would you say there are unofficial
norms, rules, expectations in the Senate, i.e., certain things members
must do and things they must not do if they want the respect and cooperation of fellow members?" If the response was affirmative, they were
also asked, "What are some of these 'rules of the game' that a member
must observe?" Every senator and every staff member responding to
the first question (96% and 95% of total interviewed, respectively)
said there were unwritten rules of the game that governed a senator's
behavior. One perceptive senator said: "Seventy percent of the Senate's
action is guided by informal rules. The Senate Rules are applied only
when the informal ones are not observed, which is rare." A staff member concurred: "Of course there are unwritten rules. I think they are
more important than the Senate Rules themselves."

Norms That Decrease Conflict

COURTESY

The observer is struck by the similarity of the Chilean Senate's folk-
ways to those described by Donald Matthews in the U.S. Senate.[12] One
group of norms reduce or set acceptable limits on partisan conflict. The
first and most widely held of this group is senatorial courtesy. Thirty-
nine (89%) of the senators responding specified twelve rules that
define this norm. The rule most frequently mentioned was, "Do not
attack other colleagues personally or be verbally aggressive." Related to
this is the practice of avoiding reference to a colleague when he is not
on the floor to defend himself. If a personal reference is unavoidable,
it is expected that the senator will advise his colleague beforehand, explain the circumstances, and give him an opportunity to prepare a
rebuttal, if necessary. One source of particular irritation is to be mis-
quoted by an opposition party senator. Avoiding this practice prevents
the animosity that could inhibit interparty cooperation. Similarly, if
understandings or compromises are ever to be reached, senators must

---

[12] Matthews, *U.S. Senators and Their World*, ch. 5.

listen to each other, ponder each other's point of view, and be sure everyone has a chance to be heard. Accordingly, senators are expected to listen patiently while others speak—on the floor and in committee.

As in the U.S. Senate, a number of formal rules aid the members in approximating expected behavior. For example, senators are expected to ask the president of the Senate for permission to speak, and to address him rather than another senator. Senators also must address each other as "Honorable" and ask permission to interrupt a speech rather than simply break in. Take this typical example of the verbal impersonality generally maintained on the floor, even when discussing such a vital issue as the 1967 constitutional reform proposal of President Frei:

> *Chadwick* [PS]. Would you permit me an interruption?
> *Aylwin* [PDC].Charged to your time.
> *Allende* [Pres.]. With the permission of Honorable Senator Aylwin, you may have the floor, Mr. Senator.
> *Chadwick* [PS]. In the speech that Honorable Senator Aylwin is making, he mentioned in passing the law creating the Ministry of Housing . . . [13]

Such occasions as re-election or retirement from the Senate are frequently used to praise a colleague publicly, across parties. One excellent example of this practice and its linkage to Chile's democratic tradition is the retirement of several senators in 1957.

> *Amunátegui* [PL]. Senator Marín [PL] has spoken kindly of Socialist Senator Eugenio González Rojas, who attends the Senate today for the last time. These kind words give prestige to the Senate and to our democracy. I think, then, that this occasion of our parliamentary life would not be complete if we didn't pay homage . . . to those other Senators who will not be with us . . . all of them fulfilled their duties with honor . . . be it on the floor, or in the active, silent, and efficient work of the committees, they served their ideas and their parties.
> *González M.* [PR]. The conduct of the Senate this afternoon and in the previous session of recognizing the accomplishments of Senators who will not continue with us is a page of democratic dignity . . . that serves

[13] *Diario de sesiones del senado, legislatura extraordinaria*, sesión 87a, February 23, 1967, p. 4264.

as an example. This is what enables us to get along together, and this is how Chilean democracy aspires and lives.[14]

Donald Matthews noted that a cardinal rule of U.S. Senate courtesy is that political disagreements should not influence personal feelings.[15] If we could find evidence for the existence of a similar rule in the Chilean Senate, it would indicate an environment conducive to interparty cooperation. One means of quantifying the Senate "culture" is to ask senators whether they get along well across parties. Senators were asked, "Would you say that senators who are members of opposing political parties get along well personally?" *Every* senator who answered (forty-three, or 96%) felt their colleagues got along well together. One senator explained: "We sign a pact of gentlemen when we enter the Senate. You can't live fighting every minute." A second senator noted: "It is characteristic of Chilean parliamentary style that no matter how the debate goes, it does not alter personal friendships and treatment. Chile is not like other Latin American countries—hate is not strong here—we are all friends." A third added: "Yes, we are very friendly and cordial here. It is an exceptional case when senators do not get along well, and then it is because someone has an unpleasant personality, not because of his political ideas."

Many senators were schoolmates together or have served in Congress approximately the same length of time. Contacts outside the Senate are regular, including family cocktails or parties, and cross-party marriages are not uncommon. The product of these interpersonal contacts and family ties is a friendly and cordial atmosphere reminiscent of a private club. Indeed, one staff member pointed out: "The Senate is a club. Students from other countries who are Communists cannot understand our Communist party members; they are conservative and flexible. Here, senators are all good friends." Another highly experienced staff member agreed: "Senators know they have to live together for eight years. They have to get along in committees or other situations.

---

[14] *Diario de sesiones del senado, legislatura extraordinaria*, sesión 18a, April 14, 1957, pp. 525–526.
[15] Matthews, *U.S. Senators and Their World*, p. 97.

The only way to live together for such a long period is to be friendly."

This is not to say that senators are always on the best of terms or that the norm of partisanship does not overpower the norm of courtesy periodically. For example, one Christian-Democrat senator noted that the early post-election period in 1965 was characterized by a high level of partisanship. "Things were really touchy in 1965. We felt strong, proud, and perhaps we made some mistakes as a result." But he continued, "Yet, over time, we have become more friendly." Curiously, several respondents called attention to the fact that personal animosity between senators is more frequently an intraparty than an interparty phenomenon. Well known are the personal feuds that separate Allende and Ampuero (PS) or the "two Humbertos" in the Radical party (Aguirre and Enríquez). But, on the whole, courtesy and other norms that reduce conflict provide and maintain a culture that allows the Senate structure of influence to make decisions without the institution collapsing. Senator Von Mühlenbrock put it this way in a memorable 1967 speech: "He who yesterday was your worst enemy, tomorrow may be your best friend."[16]

RECIPROCITY

In view of the high level of interparty friendship in the Senate, it is not surprising to find a widely held norm of reciprocity, which also helps to reduce conflict. Eighty-two percent (thirty-five) of the senators responding mentioned sixteen different rules to define this norm, which govern several stages of legislative activity. In exchange-theory terms, the norm of reciprocity prescribes that a senator should provide assistance wherever he can in full expectation that he will be repaid in kind.

Several rules govern committee work. One common rule requires a regular member to step down temporarily to allow a fellow party member to watch over and vote for a bill he has authored or one that directly affects the interests of his district. A related rule is that a senator who is not a member of a particular committee should be al-

---

[16] *Diario de sesiones del senado, legislatura extraordinaria*, sesión 87a, February 23, 1967, p. 4281.

lowed to attend sessions and even participate in the debate of a committee when a bill is of concern to him. Similarly, when a member of a committee requests that certain groups be called to testify on a bill, the president of the committee is expected to do so, even if the request comes from an opposition senator. On occasions, a member of one party may not be able to attend a committee session. If a vote is coming up that day, he will leave his vote "in trust" with another member. The trustee is expected to vote the same way the senator himself would have.

On the floor, a group of rules encourages interparty cooperation for passing certain types of legislation. One rule is that senators should vote for a bill that aids another's district whenever possible. Similarly, all five senators from the same district (even if they are members of opposing parties) are expected to work together to draw up and pass legislation that will benefit their common district. A related rule calls for senators to sign a senator's petition to bring to the floor an amendment killed in committee, even if they personally oppose it then or later on the floor. For various reasons, senators of opposing parties pair votes as in the U.S. Congress. Breaking such an agreement is one of the most severe breaches of trust a senator can make.

This system of rules is held together by the recognition of most senators that they may need another senator's support some day. Furthermore, if one senator upsets this system of mutual accommodation, a chain reaction may be set off that can touch the interests of each of them. We noted earlier that one of the ways the Senate initiates legislation is by attaching amendments on bills that the executive has classified as urgent. Both the president of the Senate and the respective committee presidents have the authority to rule out amendments on the grounds that they are not pertinent to the bill or are unconstitutional. But Senate norms prescribe that this prerogative be exercised sparingly and on a nonpartisan basis. If one committee president backed by a majority bloc vote begins to violate this norm, retaliation may be taken in another committee where the balance of votes is not the same. Or a floor leader may refuse to go along on a unanimous consent measure in interparty conference.

Matthews found in the U.S. Senate that this game works best when senators are able to visualize legislation in national terms.[17] If we could find evidence that Chilean senators do fill the role of national representatives, it would help explain how senators cooperate and compromise across parties. We sought to discover whether this role orientation exists by asking, "What do you think the role of the Senate should be in Chile's political system?" Of the twenty-nine senators responding to this question (66% of those interviewed), the overwhelming majority (twenty-six, or 90%) thought the body should have as its main role that of representing the national interest.[18] Several also perceived a conflict between this orientation and that of party or district representative, and indicated that they resolve it on particular issues by voting for the national interest as they see it.

A survey of Senate debates supports interview response. For example, Christian-Democrat Senate President Tomás Reyes (1965–1966) called members' attention to this passage of President Frei's first message to Congress in 1965: "There [in the Senate] I learned, in grand debates, that more important than partisan positions is a spirit that is in the root of our history, and that permits us to overcome differences when national interests are involved."[19] In another instance, Senator Hernán Videla (PL), as he stepped down from the presidency of the Senate, reminded his colleagues of their national role. "We have the obligation to contribute to the respect of and esteem for the Senate, because in this way we contribute to the future of the Nation."[20] Or take the 1961 speech of Senator Ampuero (PS), member of one of the supposedly more disciplined Chilean political parties. Opposing a change to Senate Rules that would give political party leadership greater control over individual senators, Ampuero noted that it had been traditional in the Senate, unlike the Chamber, to allow a more free and open debate in search of the course of action that was in the national

---

[17] Matthews, *U.S. Senators and Their World*, p. 101.

[18] The remaining three respondents wanted either to end the Senate and form a unicameral system or to make widespread structural changes of the present arrangement.

[19] *Diario de sesiones del senado, legislatura ordinaria*, sesión 1a, June 1, 1965, p. 12.

[20] *Diario de sesiones del senado, legislatura ordinaria*, sesión 1a, May 31, 1961, p. 20.

interest. Evidently perceiving a conflict between the national and party role orientations of a senator, Ampuero concluded: "In the Senate it has always been the custom that each senator, individually, has certain rights, a certain autonomy to participate in debates. In the Chamber, because of its partisan condition, political parties have had more influence as groups over the work of the legislature. Here, I repeat, the individuality of each senator has been respected more."[21]

It is not surprising that many senators hold a national role orientation. Former President Alessandri Palma sought to incorporate in the Constitution of 1925 the requirement that senators be elected nationally rather than regionally, and this proposal has many Senate supporters today.[22] Indeed, a reading of the records of the constitutional conventions of 1925 clearly shows that one objective for providing partial, off-year elections of the Senate, an age requirement of thirty-five (versus twenty-one for the Chamber), and a term of eight years (versus four) was to insulate the body from short-term periodic political movements to such a degree that national rather than partisan or personal electoral interests would predominate.[23] As Professor Guzmán, Chilean expert on constitutional law, testified before a Senate committee: "The Senate is a body of elders, that is to say, an entity where the passions are much more temperate. The institution is designed precisely to dampen the passion of the younger chamber or the executive who is too innovative."[24]

There is, then, a widely held (though not unanimous) consensus that a senator should consider himself, among other things, a representative of the nation. Frequently a conflict between this orientation and that of party or district service will be resolved in favor of the former. Herein lies the key to senators' capacity to reach cross-party compromises and to make individual reciprocal agreements. As one Senate

[21] *Diario de sesiones del senado, legislatura extraordinaria,* sesión 15a, November 21, 1961, p. 683.

[22] José Guillermo Guerra, *La constitución de 1925.*

[23] *Actas oficiales de las sesiones celebradas por la comisión y subcomisiones encargadas del estudio del proyecto de nueva constitución política de la república.*

[24] *Diario de sesiones del senado, legislatura extraordinaria,* sesión 87a, February 23, 1967, p. 4288.

saying goes, "Los hombres pasan, los Gobiernos caen, las instituciones quedan" (Men pass, governments fall, and institutions remain).

INSTITUTIONAL LOYALTY

A third norm that reduces partisan conflict is that of institutional loyalty. Thirty-seven percent (sixteen) of the senators responding named a total of six rules that define this norm. Senators take pride in the fact that the Senate and Congress as a whole have real influence in the political system, as compared with most other Latin American countries. They are not so presumptuous as to say the Senate is the greatest legislative and deliberative body in the world, as U.S. senators do, but they do make it known that the Chilean Senate is one of the oldest and one of the most influential. They are particularly sensitive of their relationship with the executive. One staff member observed: "If there is a confrontation with the executive, senators seem to unite, no matter what their party. That's curious, isn't it?" Indeed, Senate rules state that one duty of the president of the Senate is the protection of the prerogatives and honor of the Senate.[25] Similarly, senators like to draw comparisons between the Senate and Chamber. One senator noted: "We really work on bills here. Over in the Chamber, they have the attitude, 'Pass it on to the Senate—they will review it.' " A second senator observed: "There is a lot less mutual respect in the Chamber. Look at their debates. You can hardly think. Over here, it is much more friendly and cordial. I guess we have been around longer, things come into perspective." A prolonged staff interview generated this comment:

Yes. You know, I never really thought about it, but there is a certain amount of tension between the chambers. They are always concerned about who will preside over joint sessions. Senators have their own parking lot, and a bigger staff proportionally. I think the deputies resent that. You know, come to think of it, it's interesting that joint budget committee sessions meet in the Senate rather than the Chamber. In fact, a senator always presides.

An important committee secretary related an experience that indicates not only the existence of a norm of institutional loyalty, but also the degree to which the secretary had been socialized over the years.

[25] "Reglamento del senado," in *Manual del senado*, p. 121.

When I was interviewing congressmen for my own book, Senator —————— said to me, "Why criticize the body? I know there are a lot of problems, but all in all, it's one of the best legislatures in the world." [Later in interview] When Mexican congressmen come to Chile, they are amazed by the Senate's influence [said with obvious pride]. This is so, I think, because people feel it has a connection with Chile's stability and democratic tradition. That includes Frei, up to a point. He is reluctant to push his powers too far.

The high degree of emotional attachment to the institution among senators and staff alike is also exhibited in Senate speeches. For example, senators commemorated the one hundred and fiftieth year of Chilean congressional history in 1961 with these passages:

Pablo [PDC]. It is also certain that the power that gives character to democracy is that of Parliament. At this time, we are one of three countries in the world that can say they have a congress with 150 years of uninterrupted institutional life.[26]

Correa [PR]. In our Congress is projected the life of Chile, with its political, economic, and social differences. But all converge in an environment of mutual respect. . . . Our legislature . . . has been an impenetrable bastion of liberty.[27]

Von Mühlenbrock [PL]. Representative democracy can reside only in Congress. The sovereignty of the people can find expression only in Congress. Each party, each idea, will give and find its truth there.[28]

Even two senators of the far Left could manage these tributes:

Corvalán [PC]. . . . in the past century . . . the Parliament accomplished a labor that contributed to the formation of a democratic regime, liberal, relatively advanced for this time.[29]

Tarud [independent socialist]. This occasion should be one of collective satisfaction, in view of the fact that Chile is the only Latin American country that has a century and one-half of continuous parliamentary life.[30]

[26] *Diario de sesiones del senado, legislatura ordinaria,* sesión 14a, June 5, 1961, p. 672.
[27] *Ibid.,* p. 680.
[28] *Ibid.,* p. 684.
[29] *Ibid.,* p. 661.
[30] *Ibid.,* p. 664.

Senators' institutional loyalty is matched only by that of the Senate staff. It is traditional that senators from all political parties pay public tribute to an important staff member who is retiring. The recipient of this praise and attention normally responds with an emotional farewell that includes a recounting of memorable experiences the Senate career has given him.[31] Subsequently, past and present staff members get together on periodic social occasions to rehash past events and exchange political stories.

Of course, not every senator or staff member feels a deep loyalty to the institution. Periodically, Communist and Socialist senators have expressed a desire to form a unicameral legislature or to implement other major structural changes. Others advocate moderate reforms within the constitutional framework that exists. But it is apparent that even they are frequently deradicalized and socialized into the system after a number of years of parliamentary experience. Osvaldo Sunkel writes: "It would be no exaggeration to say the left-wing parties, including the Communist Party . . . have become incorporated into the political Establishment, and that their existence and influence depends on the maintenance of this system."[32]

Norms That Encourage Work and Specialization

LEGISLATIVE WORK

A second group of norms encourages hard work and specialization. The first of this group is the norm of legislative work. Fifty-eight percent (twenty-five) of the senators responding mentioned this norm and named ten rules to define it. Several rules apply primarily to committee work. One is that senators should try to study bills before they go to committee meetings. A former senator explained one evening after dinner, "I always studied bills before going to committee, and when I opened my mouth, I tried to make sure I knew what I was talking about." As in the U.S. Senate, overlapping committee assignments and other demands made on a senator may prevent his fulfilling this expec-

---

[31] *Diario de sesiones del senado, legislatura extraordinaria*, sesión 12a, November 2, 1960, p. 643.

[32] Osvaldo Sunkel, "Change and Frustration in Chile," in *Obstacles to Change in Latin America*, ed. Claudio Veliz, p. 132.

tation all the time. But the fact that it is a valued target to shoot for sets the tone of committee work.

Once in committee, senators are expected to dig in, discuss the bill in question, and try to come up with solutions satisfactory to all. Jorge Tapia Valdés describes the results of this process: "The Senate is the legislative body that does most to improve legislation. Generally, it modifies totally projects sent over by the Chamber, putting articles in logical order, writing them in intelligent form, taking out unnecessary or extraneous material, and so on."[33] Senators are also expected to attend committee and floor sessions regularly. We do not have data on committee attendance, but an OIS study for the period May 21, 1965, to September 18, 1966, showed that senators attend, on the average, 63 percent of the sessions held (see Table 38). This is a reasonably good performance when one takes into account other demands on their time, such as district trips and periodic election campaigns.

Part of the reason Senate debates tend to be serious and serene compared to those in the Chamber is that a series of rules defining the norm of legislative work exhort a senator to refrain from taking the floor when he has little or nothing to say that may shed new light on the subject at hand. Once he decides to speak, a senator generally receives more attention and overall respect if he fortifies his arguments with facts and figures and sticks to the subject at hand.

Personal observation and an extensive reading of Senate debates convinces me that most senators take their work seriously. Since World War II, senators have devoted more and more time to their legislative careers.[34] The Senate is in ordinary or extraordinary session virtually the year round. Increasingly, senators have become concerned about the adequacy of staff support. As a result, the last decade has seen the addition of the Office of Information, professionalization of committee staffs, and the passage of legislation that enables the Senate to get the information necessary to evaluate policy proposals. Whereas committees sessioned only one or two days a week in 1959, personal observation during 1968 indicated that this pattern has changed markedly. The staff itself has become an active force for reform. Late in 1967, all

[33] Jorge A. Tapia Valdés, *La técnica legislativa*, p. 31.
[34] Guillermo Bruna Contreras, *Estatuto de la profesión parlamentaria*.

TABLE 38: Attendance at Senate Floor Sessions,
May 21, 1965–September 18, 1966

Senator	Total Sessions Attended	% of Total
H. Aguirre	159	65
H. Ahumada	143	58
F. Alessandri[a]	66	27
S. Allende	109	44
C. Altamirano	171	70
R. Ampuero	178	72
P. Aylwin	136	55
J. Barros	129	53
L. Bossay	146	59
F. Bulnes	160	65
J. Campusano	161	65
B. Castro	190	77
C. Contreras	151	61
V. Contreras	166	68
S. Corbalán	167	68
L. Corvalán[b]	48	19
E. Curti	189	77
T. Chadwick	205	83
J. Durán	146	59
E. Enríquez	147	59
R. Ferrando	190	77
J. Foncea	189	77
R. Fuentealba	156	63
J. García	190	77
J. Gómez	176	71
E. González	179	72
R. Gormaz	118	48
R. Gumucio	183	75
P. Ibáñez[c]	97	39

SOURCE: Compiled from documents in Senate Office of Information, 1966 file.

[a] F. Alessandri had health problems during this period, which probably explains the low level of attendance.

[b] L. Corvalán is president of the Communist party and places greater emphasis on his party duties.

[c] P. Ibáñez has business interests that tend to make him a part-time senator.

Senator	Total Sessions Attended	% of Total
A. Jaramillo	156	63
R. Juliet	186	76
L. Luengo	188	77
J. Maurás	152	62
H. Miranda	139	56
J. Musalem	148	60
A. Noemí	204	83
T. Pablo	155	63
I. Palma	186	76
B. Prado	177	71
T. Reyes	191	77
A. Rodríguez	147	59
S. Sepúlveda	149	60
R. Tarud	107	44
V. Teitelboim	174	71
J. Von Mühlenbrock	147	59
Avg. Total	154	63

the secretaries of the Senate committees jointly discussed methods of strengthening standing committees and improving their work methods. Subsequently, a reform project was drafted and submitted to the Senate for consideration.[35]

SPECIALIZATION

As Chile has developed economically and socially over the last quarter-century, legislation has covered an increasingly wider range of issues and has taken on an added degree of complexity. Over the same period of time, the number of Senate committees has increased and their work loads have been augmented. A senator who sits on several committees simultaneously cannot hope to keep abreast of the developments in every one. It is not surprising that 28 percent of the senators responding named rules that define a norm of specialization.

Members from each party are assigned to committees primarily on

[35] *Informe de la comisión de funcionarios de la secretaría del senado encargada de elaborar un anteproyecto de reforma del reglamento de la corporación.*

the basis of their knowledge, experience, and interest in the subject matter of a committee. Those senators who have several key assignments tend to concentrate on the work of two or three of them. Several senators spend two or more legislative periods (four years each) on the same committee working with the same secretary. As a result, Senators Palma, Altamirano, and Bossay have become known as experts in finance matters, whereas Senators Alessandri, Bulnes, and Aylwin are known for their competence in constitutional legislation. Caucus discussions of a bill are heavily influenced by the most knowledgeable senator on that bill, who usually is the respective committee member. Once on the floor, the president of each committee usually presents and explains the report, and each party frequently follows the lead of its member senator. Senators are expected to speak out on matters in which they have a more specialized knowledge and to show deference to other senators in areas where they have little or no special competence.

APPRENTICESHIP

It would be inaccurate to say that the Chilean Senate has a norm of apprenticeship exactly comparable with that in the U.S. Senate. It does not. But certain similarities should be noted. Apprenticeship involves both the total congressional career and behavior within the Senate in particular. As to the former, we observed earlier that a typical congressional career involves several years in the Chamber followed by a transfer to the Senate. Legally, there is nothing that requires this pattern of ascent. In practice, most congressmen are expected to begin their careers in the Chamber. This affords the opportunity to learn the ropes as well as to demonstrate individual competence and judgment. Performance in the Chamber serves as one means of deciding who should be recruited as Senate candidates for each party or who should serve as party leaders.

Twenty-one percent (nine) of the senators interviewed mentioned rules that define a short period of watching and waiting once in the Senate. New senators spend anywhere from four to six months observing, speaking only infrequently. Furthermore, as noted earlier, both the Radical and Christian-Democrat parties expect new members to take less desirable committee assignments while more senior senators gravitate to the top committees. Still, a seniority system does not exist in any official sense, nor is it likely to.

Sanctions and Socialization

For a norm to exist, there must be agreement or consensus about the kinds of behavior group members should or should not sanction, and socialization mechanisms to produce adherence to these agreements.[36] We have already seen that Chilean senators hold widespread agreement on at least five of the six norms we have mentioned above (courtesy, reciprocity, institutional patriotism, legislative work, and specialization). But are there formal and informal sanctions to ensure that these norms are observed?

Formally, Senate Rules spell out a number of sanctions that the presiding officer and party floor leaders may employ. For example, the Senate norm of courtesy is defined by twelve rules. Two of these rules prescribe that a senator should not slander another or refer to him personally when he is not on the floor to defend himself. The presiding officer can meet violations with a series of sanctions ranging from ruling the offending senator out of order to the extreme of revoking his right to speak on the floor for a given period of time. If a particular senator or group of senators makes it a practice to violate these rules, floor leaders may retaliate by denying this senator or group's request for permission to complete an unfinished speech when their allotted floor time runs out. Or, in interparty conference, floor leaders may refuse to place a bill this group favors on the easy dispatch calendar. The possibilities are endless.

But, short of these formal sanctions, are there informal social sanctions that help keep behavior within acceptable limits? After asking senators if there were certain things members should not do if they wanted the respect and cooperation of their colleagues, we continued: "If a member does or says the things you mentioned, are there any methods that are used to encourage the member to stop doing so? What are they?" Response gives us a rich sample of the informal pressures applied. The main technique used is social ostracism. See these

[36] John W. Thibaut and Harold H. Kelley, *The Social Psychology of Groups*, p. 239.

comments for a sample of how the members close ranks on an offender: "He stands out like a chinaman" (*queda como chino*); "gets the
law of ice" (*la ley del hielo*); "He becomes the black eye" (*queda
como el ojo negro*); "brutal loss of prestige" (*desprestigio brutal*).
In a friendly cordial body like the Senate, the effect can be tremendous.

Another technique is to wait for the opportunity to get even. As one
senator described his sentiments, "It's an eye for an eye, and a tooth
for a tooth." This may take the form of refusing a senator's motion to
have his speech in the hour of incidental matters published in volume
for public distribution. Or, a senator might quote on the floor, "Senator ———'s statements regarding my personal character on the floor
of the Senate add neither to his prestige nor to that of this honorable
body." Senators may even refuse to pair with the offender or to vote
for his amendments in committee. If the behavior persists, the senator
will simply lose his colleagues' respect. One senator noted: "Well, if
this kind of thing continued on very long, he would certainly lose respect. His views would be discounted, and no one would give him
much attention. But we seldom ever reach that extreme."

The pressure of institutional norms combined with prolonged congressional careers appears eventually to socialize the most disruptive
members into the group. One concerned Socialist senator, Carlos Altamirano, writes: "Unfortunately, as a result of the tasks a legislator
must perform and the spirit of life Congress imposes, a professional
congressman is created who is the antithesis and negation of what an
authentic revolutionary agitator should be. This system of gradual and
subtle assimilation unconsciously transforms one into support of the
status quo versus being against it.[37] Clearly, another interpretation of
this socialization process is that it produces an environment that facilitates interparty cooperation and change, but at a pace the political,
economic, and social system can accommodate.

SUMMARY AND CONCLUSIONS

The Chilean Senate is guided in part by formal rules, past precedents, and the Constitution. The Senate Rules govern most day-to-day

[37] Carlos Altamirano, "El parlamento, 'tigre de papel,'" *Punto Final* 2, no. 55
(May 21, 1968): 5.

operations of the Senate and may be divided by subject into four groups: committees, sessions and calendars, control of debate, and voting. Rules require most bills to be assigned to committees according to content and further specify that all bills that involve expenditures or taxes not contained in the annual budget must clear the Finance Committee. Although floor leaders may set time limits for committees to report out bills, this is not a common practice. Furthermore, on urgency legislation, these leaders often force the president of the republic to give committees more time to study bills.

The Senate works virtually the year round. The calendar of regular sessions (May 21 to September 18) is divided into two periods: (1) reading of the minutes and reports, easy dispatch calendar, and major legislation on the order of the day calendar, and (2) incidental matters. Rules specify which bills have preference on the calendar, and floor leaders together with the president of the Senate agree on the order of remaining bills. During the hour of incidental matters, each party is allowed time to speak, proportionate to its seats in the Senate, on whatever issue it wishes to raise.

Floor debates are controlled by two sets of rules: those which promote order and decorum and those which help expedite business. The president of the Senate and the floor leaders set voting procedures on a bill. Votes may be public or secret, voice or individual roll call. Pairing is also used.

These formal procedural rules help explain how conflict is contained and business dispatched, but they do not fully explain how opposing political parties can reach a majority consensus on key legislation necessary for the stable development of the country. This turns our attention to the informal rules of the game. We find five separate Senate norms function to reduce partisan conflict and encourage identification with national program goals: courtesy, reciprocity, institutional patriotism, legislative work, and specialization. These norms are reinforced by mechanisms of socialization and sanction. There is an apprenticeship norm that governs Chamber-Senate career patterns and internal Senate behavior. However, aside from some similarities, it is not comparable to the U.S. Senate norm.

8. Conclusion

REVOLUTIONS ARE MORE LIKELY to occur when two conditions coincide: (1) political institutions incapable of providing channels for the participation of new social forces in politics and of new elites in government, and (2) social forces, currently excluded from politics, desiring to participate therein.[1] As Samuel P. Huntington notes, "Ascending or aspiring groups and rigid or inflexible institutions are the stuff of which revolutions are made."[2] One of the most neglected facts about successful great revolutions is that they have *not* occurred in democratic political systems.[3] This suggests that, on the average, democracies have developed a greater capacity for (1) assimi-

[1] Samuel P. Huntington, *Political Order in Changing Societies*, p. 274.
[2] *Ibid.*, p. 275.
[3] *Ibid.*

lating new social groups and elites desiring to participate in politics, and (2) providing mechanisms for the processing of their demands into meaningful outputs.

Several institutions appear to generate this capacity in the Chilean political system and thus have played a part in the country's long history of political stability.[4] We have focused our attention on one of these institutions—the Chilean Senate. One reason for describing and analyzing the internal distribution of influence of the Chilean Senate was to determine how, specifically, the Senate contributes to Chile's political stability. In conclusion, we will seek to describe some of the ways suggested by our exploratory research.[5]

MANAGEMENT OF CONFLICT

Chile is a pluralistic political system subject to a variety of stresses and group conflicts. The gap between the social classes, the regressive effects of high rates of inflation (25 to 30% annually), and the competition between the heavily populated central zone and the more recently colonized southern zone over scarce government resources are just some examples. If the total political system is to persist, it must provide various arenas in which these conflicts can be resolved.

One of the most important arenas is the Chilean Senate. There are at least four ways in which the Senate contributes to the management of conflict: deliberation, decision-making, adjudication, and catharsis.

Deliberation

One of the unique features of the Senate (versus most other Chilean political institutions) that reduces conflict and generates support for the total political system is that it represents the *only* access point where *all* the major political parties and interest groups can meet and have

---

[4] For example, see James Petras, *Politics and Social Forces in Chilean Development*, for a discussion of the role of the bureaucracy, and Federico G. Gil, *The Political System of Chile*, ch. 6, for a discussion of the role of political parties.

[5] The following discussion was influenced by a reading of Malcolm E. Jewell and Samuel C. Patterson, *The Legislative Process in the United States*, pp. 8–15; and Leon N. Lindberg, "The Role of the European Parliament in an Emerging European Community," in *Lawmakers in a Changing World*, ed. Elke Frank, especially pp. 121–123.

their voices heard on pending legislation or other key issues of the day. For example, the bureaucracy does not provide adequate access to leftist interests or political parties.[6] Similarly, because the government party (PDC) had a majority in the Chamber from 1965 to 1969, bills were rapidly dispatched without adequate consideration of the views of other political parties or interests. Since the government did not have a majority in the Senate, however, the body stood as the last bastion where opposition political parties and interest groups could force the executive to allow more time for a hearing on their views in standing committees and on the floor. As Jewell and Patterson note, "It is symptomatic of the essential part the legislative system plays in managing conflict that, if the legislature becomes a rubber stamp or a law factory, there may be no other arena in which adequate deliberation is possible."[7]

The formal and informal procedures within the Senate also serve the purpose of ensuring that there will be time and opportunity for a variety of interests and viewpoints to be heard. For example, each of the five major political parties (National, Radical, Christian-Democrat, Socialist, and Communist) are represented not only on the floor, but also in all the influential standing committees. The bloc apportionment system also gives each party the opportunity to chair some committees. Such norms as reciprocity and tolerance give major interest groups minimum assurance that their views on important bills will be heard during committee hearings. Similarly, committee and Office of Information staffs are expected to be on call to all political parties. On the floor, formal and informal rules allow each political party time to debate proportionate to its strength in the Senate. Furthermore, provincial election of senators assures a minimum voice for regional interests. Together these minimum guarantees of access and participation facilitate acceptance of the Senate's final decisions and thus hold conflict to a minimum.

---

[6] Petras, *Politics and Social Forces*, ch. 8. Although the bureaucracy probably does represent a fusion of modern and traditional values, it appears to be dominated by members of the Radical, Christian-Democrat, and National parties. Access to the Socialist and Communist parties seems imperfect.

[7] Jewell and Patterson, *The Legislative Process*, p. 10.

The deliberative process in the Senate also restrains conflict by defining and transmitting in its debates and other activities a concept of the general interest of the nation as a whole. This makes members (and citizens on the periphery) feel that they are a part of a larger historical process that calls for personal and partisan restraint on behalf of future benefits.[8] The overwhelming majority of the senators interviewed thought that the main role of the Senate is to represent the national interest. As an example, we noted earlier that Socialist Senator Ampuero objected to greater national political party control over senators because it had been traditional in the Senate, unlike the Chamber, to allow more free and open debates in search of a course of action that was in the national interest.

Frequently, a conflict between this national role orientation and that of party or district service will be resolved in favor of the former—thereby enabling senators to make cross-party compromises and individual reciprocal agreements. President Frei's first message to Congress in 1965, quoted before, gives testimony to this fact: "There [in the Senate], I learned, in grand debates, that more important than partisan positions is a spirit that is in the root of our history, and that permits us to overcome differences when national interests are involved."[9]

Decisional

The Senate exercises considerable influence in the Chilean political system, and public opinion (based on a 1965 random sample of Santiago residents taken at a time when President Frei's support was probably at its apex) appears to support Congress's demands for a powerful voice in the policy-making process. As is the case with its deliberative function, public support for the Senate is linked to the fact that the body often represents the only governmental institution where all the major political parties and interest groups may make and have some of their important demands met. By hearing, mediating, moderating, and refining these competing demands, the Senate helps to resolve conflict

[8] For a discussion of this process, see David Easton, *A Systems Analysis of Political Life*, p. 273.
[9] *Diario de sesiones del senado, legislatura ordinaria*, sesión 1a, June 1, 1965, p. 12.

and to avoid alienating key groups that might be dysfunctional to the operation and persistence of the total political system.[10]

For example, both the business community on the Right and unions on the Left are represented in the Senate. Data indicated that, just as the Right attempts to chair the standing committees of Finance or Economy and Commerce, the Left shows interest in Labor and Social Legislation or Public Health. Colonization of the presidencies of different committees ensures competing interests access, "permitting a balance of forces, more facts, and resolution with greater clarity."[11] In contrast, legislation initiated by the executive branch, as it is first submitted to Congress, and the Christian-Democrat–dominated Chamber's review of such legislation frequently do not provide for or reflect a similar consideration and balancing of the country's diverse interests. A 1967 *New York Times* editorial gives evidence of this fact: ". . . Chileans, whom many consider the most democratic of all Latin Americans, are accustomed to the adjustments and the give-and-take of party politics. In the Frei regime they faced a stiffness that many considered to be arrogance."[12]

Accordingly, one of the many significant ties of the Senate to Chile's overall political stability and long democratic tradition appears to be its exercise of decisional influence to initiate legislation and force the executive to modify his bills in order to meet more adequately the demands of a wider group of competing interests. This process benefits groups on the Left as well as on the Right.[13]

[10] For the importance of this process, see Huntington, *Political Order in Changing Societies*, pp. 9, 167, 196.

[11] Jorge A. Tapia Valdés, *La técnica legislativa*, p. 41.

[12] "Another Blow to President Frei," *New York Times*, April 17, 1967, p. 26.

[13] There is a growing consensus among scholars that legislatures in the developing nations are more conservative than the executive (e.g., see Huntington, *Political Order in Changing Societies*, pp. 388–389; and Robert Packenham, "Legislatures and Political Development," in *Legislatures in Developmental Perspective*, ed. Allan Kornberg and Lloyd D. Musolf. They are inclined to perceive congressional delays or modifications of executive bills as undue harassment that works to the advantage of interests on the Right. Although this may be a valid generalization for most of Latin America and may also be applicable to the Chilean Senate in earlier periods of the country's history, it is not entirely clear that this generalization is valid for the Chilean Senate today.

The 1968 Salary Readjustment Bill provides a good example. Through this bill, President Frei attempted, in effect, to tax public employees by offering them a salary increase that was somewhat less than the previous year's rate of inflation. Political parties and interest groups on the Left opposed the bill because they felt it worked to the disadvantage of public employees, particularly those at the lowest income levels. Because the government party (PDC) had a majority in the Chamber, the bill was rapidly dispatched without consideration of the views of other political parties. The government did not have a majority in the Senate, however, which thus represented the only access point where opposition parties (and interest groups) could make their voices heard and have their demands partially met. By forcing the executive to accept amendments, the Senate reached a compromise solution that permitted passage of the bill while avoiding the complete alienation of groups on the Left.

It should also be noted that executive bills are not always perfect or desirable for adoption. In a rush to create an image of "action" that will generate support in the next by-election, new administrations (representing both the Right and the Left) often submit a myriad of projects to Congress that have not been adequately or carefully analyzed for the full implications of their enactment. By forcing the executive in these instances to allow the Senate enough time to consider the implications of these proposed bills, the Senate performs a real service for the nation by improving the laws it modifies or delays (e.g., reordering and rewriting bills so that they are clear and understandable) and by refusing to pass those bills which might push group conflicts beyond controllable bounds. As Professor Guzmán, Chilean expert on constitutional law at the University of Chile, notes, this is precisely the role defined for the Senate by the Constitution of 1925—"to act as a brake on the passions of the Chamber and an overly innovative President,"[14] whether it signifies a movement to the Left or to the Right.

Take the University Reform Law of 1968, for example. President Frei had classified the bill urgent, thereby requiring consideration within thirty days. The bill sailed through the Christian-Democrat-

[14] *Diario de sesiones del senado, legislatura extraordinaria,* sesión 87a, February 23, 1967, p. 4288.

dominated Chamber and was sent on to the Senate. In the Senate, however, the political parties' leadership argued that a bill of such importance could not be responsibly considered in the time limit allowed and
forced the executive to provide adequate time for its study (or to face
rejection). In May, 1968, the representatives (*comités*) of the Communist, Christian-Democrat, Radical, and Socialist parties issued this
public statement: "The representatives declare that the project contains
matters of great importance that require study and careful legislation.
. . . The periods for a petition of urgency are insufficient to make such
a study. . . . In view of this, we have asked the minister of education
. . . to ask the president to retire the urgency. . . . and we indicated
that a period of sixty days was a prudent and legitimate period to study
the initiative, obtain all the relevant data, and hear the opinions of the
authorities of the universities."[15]

Also contributing to the entire political system's capacity to resolve
conflict is the Senate's role as one of the most effective institutional
arenas for dampening the partisanship accentuated elsewhere in the
political system (e.g., in the Chamber of Deputies and the various
political parties) and for encouraging agreements and compromises
among opposing political parties. This not only makes majority decisions possible (which in turn generates specific support for the total
political system), but may also encourage the development of similar
habits and norms in other parts of the political system.

The committee system with its intermediate level of independence
from national political party leadership is probably the single most important mechanism for encouraging the formation of interparty majority
agreements. Assignment of bills to specialized subject-matter committees helps to break controversies down into a manageable size. Senate
conference recruitment (for all the political parties except the Communist party) emphasizes criteria of expertise, specialization, constituency characteristics, senators' preferences, and past committee service,
together with a closed-door, off-the-record committee environment, reinforced by the highly trained nonpartisan staff. This emphasis tends

---

[15] *Declaración de los comités comunista, demócrata cristiano, radical, y socialista
del senado en relación con el estudio del proyecto que legisla sobre las universidades,*
n.d.

to discourage partisan exchanges between senators and to focus attention on how to satisfy conflicting demands over a given bill. Here,
senators are encouraged to weigh the broad national interest against
partisan demands—which often leads to interparty compromises and
agreements (outputs).

Interparty cooperation and compromise is also fostered through
components of the legislative leadership structure. For example, interparty conferences consisting of floor leaders representing all the senators take place regularly before floor sessions (and on other occasions)
in order to work out mutually acceptable agreements on the floor calendar, debates, and other interparty matters. These meetings are characterized by pragmatic bargaining rather than by ideological impasse because Senate expectations of floor leaders emphasize cooperation and
work over partisanship. Interparty conferences are closed and off the
record. And, in the search for mutually acceptable agreements, the
president of the Senate acts as a catalyst by the nonpartisan manner in
which he presides over these meetings (as well as floor debates).

The capacity of senators to contain disruptive conflict, to reach interparty agreements, and to identify with the national interest also seems
to be closely linked to formal and informal Senate rules. For example,
the number of areas of potential conflict is reduced by formal Senate
rules covering such crucial areas as committee meetings, sessions and
calendars, debates, and voting and by informal rules of courtesy, reciprocity, and institutional patriotism. Similarly, norms of legislative
work and specialization focus committee deliberations and floor debates
on resolving conflict.

Adjudication

Adjudication routines are frequently performed by the Chilean Senate. The Senate has power to perform quasi-judicial functions, such as
interpreting the Constitution as it relates to particular bills, ruling on
the interpretation of Senate Rules, and deciding cases of censure of
ministers of state, senators, and mayors. As a rule, the Senate Committee of Constitution, Legislation, Justice, and Rules, which reports on
these matters, sets a responsible nonpartisan example in its review that
is normally followed on the floor. As a result, few impeachment cases

are approved, but if sufficiently justified, the committee will vote otherwise, as happened on several occasions during the unpopular Ibáñez administration (1952–1958).

Jewell and Patterson note that much of the private-bill process in the U.S. Congress is largely adjudicative in nature, in the sense that individual grievances (conflicts between individuals and the authorities) are settled thereby.[16] A similar process exists in the Chilean Senate. Jorge Tapia Valdés points out that 55.2 percent of the laws passed by Congress between 1938 and 1958 were over particular matters— pensions, jobs, or retirement benefits (*asuntos de gracia*)—in response to demands made but not satisfied in the bureaucracy.[17]

Finally, while overseeing the administration, Senate standing committees' activities and floor debates have on occasion been trials, in effect, during the course of which sanctions (formal or informal) have been applied. For example, a review in 1967 of administration policies inspired the Senate to refuse President Frei permission to travel to the United States.

Catharsis

The Senate cannot accede to the demands of all interests, sometimes not even partially, but it can grant these interests a hearing perhaps not obtainable in the bureaucracy or the Chamber of Deputies. This hearing can be an important factor in controlling conflict as well as a means of generating wide support for the total political system. Take committee hearings and floor debates, for example. Political parties and groups of both the far Right and the far Left continually air demands that cannot practically be met (e.g., to end agrarian reform or to nationalize the copper mines completely). But the very process of offering conflicting interests an opportunity to let off steam and clear the air releases tensions sufficiently to allow discussion of substantive issues.[18] Furthermore, these debates may also serve the government as a bellwether or

---

[16] Jewell and Patterson, *The Legislative Process*, p. 12.

[17] Tapia Valdés, *La técnica legislativa*, p. 47.

[18] For a discussion of this process as it relates to unrealistic versus realistic conflict and to communal and noncommunal conflict, see Lewis A. Coser, *The Functions of Social Conflict*, particularly pp. 44, 49–50, 75, 81–82.

warning device as to the directions in which it must move to maintain national stability.

INTEGRATION OF THE TOTAL POLITICAL SYSTEM

The Chilean political system is subject to a variety of stresses. If the total political system is to endure, it must be able to cope with such stress. This presumes a minimum level of system-wide integration. The Chilean Senate helps to provide this level of integration by generating specific and widespread support for the total political system and by providing institutional mechanisms for reducing diversity. This is accomplished in four specific ways: representation, authorization, legitimation, and socialization.

Representation

The Chilean Senate contributes to the support of the polity first of all by virtue of its representative character. A proportional representation system is used in congressional elections in an effort to assure that all shades of political opinion have at least a minimum representation in the Senate. All five major political parties are represented not only on the floor, but also in each of the influential standing committees. Furthermore, each party has an opportunity to chair some committees, and formal and informal rules provide that each political party has time for debate in proportion to its strength in the Senate. These mechanisms have enabled the Senate to serve as an effective opposition site, thereby encouraging all political parties (including the PS and PC) to work through and identify with the total political system. This characteristic of the Senate has no doubt helped to maintain the relative stability of Chile's multiparty system.

Also significant is the fact that the Senate successfully blends the representation of group, regional, and national interests, which aids national integration and the persistence of the political system. At the group level, senators are directly linked to and represent both the business and labor community. Regionally, senators are elected by a group of provinces (*agrupaciones*), directly by the people. As in the United States, senators maintain frequent contact with their *agrupación* and have on occasion voted against their party in preference to regional interests. Regional election and representation also appear to be a useful mechanism for reconciling conflict between societal and regional interests, thereby enabling the system to endure. One senator argues, "With our unitary system, which tends toward control from Santiago, and, at the same time, regions with such diverse characteristics and needs, direct representation by *agrupación* is necessary." Finally, some senators prefer to define their role as representing the national interest, at times acting as a brake (*freno*) on the Chamber. They contend that the objective of partial election of senators is to encourage a national versus regional view on issues.

"A state without the means of some change," Edmund Burke observed of the French Revolution, "is without the means of its conservation."[19] The Senate appears to have generated public support for the total political system precisely because it has demonstrated the capacity and willingness to improve its representational character over the years. One measure is the career background of the Senate membership in 1965, compared with 1933; representation has moved away from military and rural interests toward a broader, more truly representative base. Responding to demands for better representation in Congress for the southern zone of Chiloé, Aisén, and Magallanes, senators from ideologically opposed political parties supported a constitutional reform that created in 1969 a tenth *agrupación* and raised the total number of senators from forty-five to fifty.[20]

Finally, the Senate also contributes to the support of the total political system by providing a unique institutional arena in Chile where all the representatives of the various participants in the legislative process may interact and have their views heard and mediated. An interest group usually represents only limited interests. The executive normally represents only the political forces dominant in the polity at one time. The administrator represents just a segment of the bureaucracy, and the party leader represents only one shade of public opinion. The Senate, however, acts as a forum where all these special interests may interact

[19] Cited in Huntington, *Political Order in Changing Societies*, p. 19.
[20] For the Senate debates on this proposal, see *Diario de sesiones del senado, legislatura ordinaria*, sesiones 13, 34, 39, 47–50, 52–53, August, 1966, and seven in June, 1967.

and provides the institutional environment to encourage the resolution of their differences.

Authorization and Legitimation

The Senate also helps to integrate the political system by authorization and legitimation. The Senate (along with the Chamber, in certain cases) must approve the annual budget, diplomatic, military, and cabinet appointments, international treaties and agreements, and permission for the president of the republic to leave the country, and it may also grant extraordinary powers to the executive in emergency situations. When the Senate gives agents of government the permission to act (authorization), the body's constitutional and traditional authority and the orderly procedures that it follows legitimate the actual exercise of authority by the governmental agents. It is regarded by the public as right and proper.

The importance of this function can be illustrated by the consequences of the Senate's questioning the legitimacy of government activities. Take the reform of Article 10, Section 10, of the Constitution, for example.[21] On matters of constitutional reform, the president may not use the additive veto (add totally new pieces of legislation), as with normal bills. President Frei attempted to use the additive veto on this reform bill, and the Senate refused to consider the veto, arguing that it was additive and therefore unconstitutional according to Article 109 of the Constitution. Frei subsequently sent another constitutional reform bill to Congress, which called for allowing the president to dissolve Congress once during his term. After rapid passage in the Christian-Democrat–dominated Chamber, the bill died on February 23, 1967, in the Senate.[22] The president then attempted to stamp the April, 1967, municipal elections as a plebiscite in support of his program and confidently predicted a plurality of 40 percent. "A vote against the party is a vote against the government" was the slogan.[23] It proved a

[21] "Senado versus Frei: Constitución puesta a prueba," *Ercilla*, December 14, 1966, pp. 4–5.

[22] "Rechazo de reforma," *El Mercurio*, February 26, 1967, p. 17.

[23] Alejandro Cabrera Ferrada, "Voz y silencio de las cifras," *Ercilla*, April 5, 1967, p. 1.

grave miscalculation. Although the Christian-Democrat percentage (36.5%) rose from the 1963 municipal election total of 22.8 percent, it fell far short of the expected 40 percent.

Socialization

One of the most important contributions the Chilean Senate makes to the stability of the total political system is the institutional mechanisms it provides for socializing ideologically opposed members to identify with and support the total political system. Samuel P. Huntington notes significance of this function:

Where the political system lacks autonomy, [new] groups gain entry into politics without becoming identified with the established political organizations or acquiescing in the established political procedures. . . . Conversely, in a developed political system the autonomy of the system is protected by mechanisms that restrict and moderate the impact of new groups. These mechanisms either slow down the entry of new groups into politics or, through a process of political socialization, impel changes in the attitudes and behavior of the most politically active members of the new group.[24]

CONCLUSION

After a number of years of parliamentary experience and exposure to institutional norms in the Senate, senators in all political parties come to take great pride in the facts that Congress is one of the oldest and most influential legislatures in the world and that the Senate often improves bills sent over by the executive branch. They also see that the Senate is frequently the only place where a president is forced to consider the views of opposition political parties and interest groups, and that this process is important to Chile's political development and stability. As a result, most senators (who are often also national party leaders) seek to work through the political system, even if immediate demands are not always satisfactorily met.

In view of the 1969 amendments to the constitution, which, on paper, seem to strengthen the power of the president of the republic at the expense of Congress, and in view of the recent election of Presi-

[24] Huntington, *Political Order in Changing Societies*, p. 21.

dent Salvador Allende, the first Marxist ever freely elected in the world, some observers wonder if Congress, particularly the Senate, will continue to be a power in the Chilean political system and to perform the integrative functions I have discussed above. For example, some of these observers point out that one of the planks of the Communist party's election platform calls for a unicameral "people's" legislature. Many fear this means that Congress will eventually become a body that only symbolically legitimates decisions taken by the president or the political party leadership—bringing to an end Congress's vigorous exercise of decisional power.

At the time of this writing, I do not believe we have enough evidence to support this view. The research findings presented here and analysis of recent events in Chile lead me to believe that Congress— particularly the Senate—will continue to exercise important decisional influence and to perform the integrative functions described above. First of all, it must be emphasized that President Allende was elected by only 37 percent of the Chilean people. Nearly an equal number of voters supported former President Jorge Alessandri—the candidate of the far Right. Thus, it does not seem accurate to say that Allende has a strong popular mandate to implement radical reforms that include dissolution of Congress. It must also be recalled that public opinion polls cited in chapter 1 indicate widespread support for a strong Congress independent of the executive branch. These political facts of life should severely limit what President Allende can legitimately do to weaken the role of Congress.

Second, as recent reports have indicated (and my personal interviews in 1968 confirm), there are elements within President Allende's coalition (particularly factions of the Radical party) who will resist attempts to reform radically the role of Congress. Third, and perhaps most important, is the style of President Salvador Allende himself, which suggests that Allende does not personally favor and probably will not seek to weaken or close down Congress, despite campaign rhetoric to the contrary. This study clearly demonstrates that when President Allende was president of the Senate, he normally abided by role expectations that required him to preside over the Senate in a nonpartisan manner. Allende's role behavior as a senator also suggests that he may well be *more* solicitous and responsive to opposition political parties' points of view in the Senate than was characteristic of the Christian-Democrats' administration. It should also be noted that thus far President Allende has followed the constitutional rules of the game by submitting his proposed constitutional amendment on property rights (for nationalization of the copper mines) to Congress for deliberation. There has been no attempt to ignore Congress in the decision-making process. Furthermore, he has sought to make clear what I believe are his authentic views on the role of the Communist party in his administration—namely, "that the Communist party will not give the orders." As far as the Congress is concerned, this would seem to signify little change in the institution's influence in the near future.

Finally, characteristic of Chilean politics, the opposition political parties (particularly the PDC) are oiling their campaign machinery for the 1971 municipal elections because these elections are normally regarded as bellwethers of current public opinion and support. The results could sharply weaken Allende's already limited base of support and so set severe restrictions on the degree of institutional tinkering that will be accepted by the majority of the Chilean people, not to mention the Chilean military and interested foreign powers.

Epilogue

DURING THE NINE MONTHS since the election of Marxist President Salvador Allende in September, 1970, which was strengthened by the near 50 percent vote his coalition won in the municipal elections in the spring of 1971, observers of Chile have become increasingly concerned that the country's long tradition of democracy and freedom may gradually be eroded and eventually disappear altogether. There are indications that these fears may not be groundless. Consequently, I have taken the opportunity to add, at the galley stage, an overview of trends in Chile since Allende's election. Chile has been changing in the past few months, and it is in the context of these changes that speculation about the future of the Chilean Senate must be made.

Despite Allende's frequent assurances that neither he nor the members of his *Unidad Popular* Coalition plan to install a totalitarian government in Chile, several analysts, including former Christian-Democrat President Eduardo Frei Montalva, fear that the left-wing government is in fact "installing a regime that will make democracy impossible."[1] Reluctance to accept President Allende's promises at face value is due in part to contradictory statements he and other members of his coalition have made. For example, on the one hand Senator Volodia Teitelboim, one of the leading economic thinkers in the Communist party, stresses the "need to come to terms with western capital and the local bourgeoisie" and criticizes the *miristas* and radical Socialists as "men who failed to self-critize after September 4th."[2] Yet, in April, 1971, Teitelboim told an audience of dignitaries at the theater of the labor confederation in Cuba that "we know we can count on the solidarity of Cuba. From now on, our destinies march together."[3] Similarly, although Allende has said that "we do not intend to escape out of one field of gravity (United States paramountcy) only to fall into another (Russian paramountcy),"[4] Carlos Altamirano, secretary-general of the Socialist party, has been quoted as saying he plans to make Chile, after Cuba, "the second free territory of America."[5] Equally disconcerting is Allende's own apparent inconsistency. *Le Monde Weekly* quotes the president to have said: "The important thing to remember is that what we are doing in Chile is being done in the legal framework of bourgeois legislation and under a democratic, bourgeois regime. We are committed to this pro-

---

[1] Former President Frei's opinion was reported by Juan de Onis, "Orderly Chilean Election Drive Ends," *New York Times*, April 4, 1971, p. 26. Other analysts' opinions were gleaned from personal interviews conducted during the "Scholar-Diplomat Seminar on Latin America" in Washington, D.C., sponsored by the Department of State, January 11–15, 1971, and from a reading of numerous books and periodicals over the last six months. For example, see *Confidential Foreign Report* (London, England: The Economist Newspaper Limited), April 15, 1971, pp. 1–3, and "Who Got the Rabbit," *Atlas* (March, 1971), p. 6.

[2] "The New Machiavelli," *The Economist*, April 10, 1971, p. 44.

[3] Reported over the Associated Press wire service and printed, among other places, in "Castro Denounces Possible Reconciliation with U.S. and OAS," *Grand Rapids Press* in April, 1971.

[4] "Little by Little, the Real Power In Chile Is Passing into Our Hands: Interview with President Salvador Allende," *Le Monde Weekly*, February 10, 1971, p. 3.

[5] "The New Machiavelli," p. 40.

cedure and we must honor that commitment."[6] But, the April 10, 1971, issue of *The Economist* notes that Dr. Allende has made no secret of his impatience with "relics of bourgeois legality," and has called for a "people's constitution" that would provide for a single-chamber congress and people's tribunals as a means of bypassing the independent judiciary.[7]

Also revealing is the Soviet Union's call to developing countries to follow Chile's example and create united fronts of Communists and others favoring noncapitalist systems. In a recent issue of *Kommunist*, the Communist party's theoretical journal, Rostislav A. Ulyanovsky, the party's leading specialist on developing countries, said that such fronts provide opportunities to increase Communist influence gradually as the country breaks with its Western links.[8] This statement is significant when combined with the fact that Chile presently has an economic mission touring seven Eastern European countries and the Soviet Union to obtain economic aid for Chile's "construction of socialism."[9]

Although it is easy to sympathize with President Allende's humanistic goals of providing a more equitable distribution of income than exists now, and more jobs, better food, housing, education, health, rest, and recreation for the marginal groups (all consistent with the objectives of the Alliance for Progress of the 1960's), some observers think that recent events in Chile suggest that these goals will be achieved (if at all) at the expense of individual freedom and liberty. They base their opinion in part on that fact that illegal seizure of more than three hundred farms by rural laborers and peasants has been reported since Dr. Allende's government took office in November. The government has taken no police measures to prevent occupancies or to evict invaders. Dr. Jacques Chonchol, minister of agriculture, has said: "This

---

[6] "Interview with Allende," p. 3.

[7] "The New Machiavelli," p. 41. Also reported elsewhere, e.g., Joseph Kraft, "Letter from Santiago," *The New Yorker*, January 30, 1971, pp. 80–89.

[8] Bernard Gwertzman, "Soviet Calls on Developing Countries to Form United Fronts Like Chile's," *New York Times*, April 28, 1971, p. 3.

[9] Juan de Onís, "Chile Sends Trade Team to East Europe," *New York Times*, May 16, 1971, p. 13.

government cannot take up arms against the people. That would be to play into the hands of reactionaries."[10] Even though José Toha, minister of the interior, announced that the government would act vigorously against any armed groups operating in rural areas, Juan de Onís of the *New York Times* reports that in practice the government has been "appointing state administrators and providing technical assistance and credit to peasant groups that seized properties in Cautín province. The farm owners have been unable to recover their properties, even small farms of 100 acres, despite orders issued by local judges for the eviction of invaders."[11] The insecurity created by these illegal seizures is likely to bring a decline in farm production and create food shortages later in 1971.[12]

Before taking office, President Allende agreed to a series of constitutional amendments guaranteeing, among other things, freedom of the press, the right to join labor unions and to strike, and an educational system free of official intervention.[13] Although it is generally believed that Allende and the democratic factions of *Unidad Popular* who follow him are trying to respect these guarantees, there appears to be pressure from other quarters within the coalition not to take these commitments seriously. The Inter-American Press Society, composed mainly of the larger and more conservative newspapers in Latin America, has charged the Communist party cadres within the coalition of overtly threatening Chilean editors and menacing press freedom.[14] It has been confirmed that Jorge Insunza, a Communist deputy, visited several radio stations that had not supported his candidacy and pressured them to hire party members. The suspension of Radio Mineira, a pro–Christian-Democrat station, and President Allende's own personal attack on

[10] "The New Machiavelli," p. 44.

[11] Juan de Onís, "Chile to Block Farm Seizures," *New York Times*, February 14, 1971, p. 2.

[12] James Nelson Goodsell, "Shadows Overhang Chilean Economy," *Christian Science Monitor*, April 26, 1971.

[13] Norman Gall, "The Chileans Have Elected a Revolution," *New York Times Magazine*, November 1, 1970, p. 106.

[14] "El Mercurio Fights Repressive Tactics of Chilean Communists," *IAPA News*, February, 1971, p. 3.

two journalists (Raul Gonzales Alfaro and Rafael Otero) followed by cancellation of the latter's radio programs are but two more examples given.[15]

More covertly, the government also appears to have adopted a number of measures designed to bring about the economic asphyxiation of the opposition press. *El Mercurio*, the conservative daily, has almost been crippled by the loss of advertising. The strike that in November paralyzed the Zig Zag Publishing House (the most important in the country), resulting in its purchase by the government, was encouraged by the political parties and organizations of the *Unidad Popular*. Furthermore, the government has issued a weekly magazine of its own, *Ahora*, to compete with *Ercilla*, Chile's foremost news review. The latter move seems consistent with the coalition's statement that "communications media would be used for the free expression of differing points of view but also to contribute to the creation of a new culture and the rise of a new man."[16] Summarizing these developments, the special correspondent of the *Economist* writes: "Dr. Allende's strategy here has been to build up the pro-government press, to sponsor the formation of *Unidad Popular* cells in the unions of journalists and printing staff, and to count on economic factors (including the increasing importance of government advertising) to bring around some of the opposition papers or to drive them off the market."[17]

Despite the fact that the Allende forces have also promised to permit strikes, there is no indication as to how far they will allow labor disputes to go. One clue is a recent statement by Luís Corvalán, secretary-general of the Communist party. He explained that under previous non-Marxist governments, it was correct for unions to press for the highest possible wage increases. "Now that the workers have their own government," he said, "demands for increases and other aspirations should be moderated to avoid causing it problems."[18] As for educational autonomy, World Wide Information Services, Inc.'s recent report notes that

[15] *Ibid.*, p. 5.
[16] Joseph Novitski, "Chile's Papers Exercise Caution Following Election," *New York Times*, September 21, 1970, p. 3.
[17] "The New Machiavelli," p. 44.
[18] Juan de Onís, "Allende's First 100 Days: The Socialism is Low Key," *New York Times*, February 15, 1971, p. 8.

Allende's government has started to revise some promises made during the election campaign last year: "Notwithstanding the fact that Allende promised an educational system free of official intervention, the Ministry of Education has brought twenty-four specialists from Cuba to give advice in the reorientation of the Chilean educational system."[19] It has also been alleged that the Ministry of Education has begun textbook revisions in the social sciences—especially in the school for teachers. In response to charges that Allende intended to close the French *lycée* in Santiago, he responded: "But why should we close it? In the morning it would give courses for paying students and in the afternoon lessons would be free, for the people . . ."[20]

The future of the Chilean economy, according to *Christian Science Monitor* correspondent James Nelson Goodsell, is also uncertain. Copper production is slowing down while world market prices also weaken, and nationalization legislation is likely to be approved by Congress by mid-1971.[21] The amount of compensation to be paid to American companies is not clear, however, and President Allende has threatened not to sign the bill unless the lower house of Congress reconsiders the composition of the five-man compensation tribunal to provide for greater government representation.[22] The official jobless total now is over 9 percent (some unofficial estimates place the total between 15 and 20%) due to a slump in the construction industry and a lag in government work projects.

The economic strategy of Pedro Vuskovic Bravo, minister of economy, has been based primarily not on sweeping expropriations, but on indirect manipulation of prices, wages, and credit, plus administrative pressures and inducements that are bringing all important private business as well as banking activities under the control of state planners. Prices of consumer goods as well as raw materials have been frozen while wage increases of 35 to 60 percent for workers have been allowed. In cases of arbitration of wage disputes, the government has

[19] Reported in "Chilean Economic Policies Receive Harsh Judgment," *The Times of the Americas*, Vol. XV, No. 12, March 24, 1971, p. 3.
[20] "Interview with Allende," p. 3.
[21] Goodsell, "Shadows Overhang Chilean Economy."
[22] *Latin America*, May 21, 1971, p. 168.

taken the side of unions. The government also refuses to permit layoffs, and the few plants that have tried or have suspended production have been taken over by a state administrator and a workers' council.

Many business leaders believe that eventually all private business will be organized along lines laid down by the State Planning Board and the State Development Corporation. With private banking being taken over by the state as well, there will be no independent source of credit, so it will disappear. Vuskovic and Orlando Letelier (Chile's ambassador to the United States) deny that the government plans to condemn the private sector to death, but they do admit that the government wants to lessen its influence within a three-pronged economic establishment of state, mixed, and private sectors.[23] Dr. Allende himself has made clear his desire to "socialize the Chilean economy."[24]

Uncertain as to what the government's long-run plans are, key personnel (both foreign and Chilean) have left or are in the process of secretly leaving the country, and the U.S. government has received an abnormally large number of requests for asylum in this country. Attempting to stem this flow, the Chilean government has placed a 30 percent premium on the cost of purchasing foreign exchange to take abroad.

In all fairness to the present administration, it should be noted that there are observers who scoff at the possibility that Allende would restrict freedom in Chile. Selden Rodman, a veteran Latin American observer, reports that, although Edward M. Korry (the former U.S. ambassador to Chile) is pessimistic about the country's future, he still characterizes Allende as a "populist" and a "humanist."[25] The Peace Corps is said to regard the president as "a democrat at heart, firmly committed to carrying out vital social changes with a maximum of freedom."[26] Some also believe that Allende himself opposes the creation of a socialist dictatorship for fear that the Community party, with its

[23] Olcutt Sanders, "Letelier Says Chile Has Full Freedom of Dialog," *The Times of the Americas*, May 5, 1971, p. 3.

[24] See Joseph Novitski, "Allende, in an Interview, Rejects Totalitarian Rule," *New York Times*, October 4, 1970, p. 1.

[25] Selden Rodman, "April in Chile: Turning Point for Allende," *New Leader*, April 5, 1971, p. 9, and personal interviews.

[26] *Ibid.*

superior organization and control of the labor movement, would become the real boss.[27] They also point out that Allende has granted asylum not only to *guerrilleros* of Brazil and Bolivia, but also to twenty-five rightist military officers from Bolivia who fled their country after trying to overthrow Torres. Rodman adds that some *comerciantes* were somewhat reassured in the fall of 1970 when top editors of Chile's number two Communist newspaper, *Puro Chile*, were promptly jailed for openly advocating defiance of the law in the matter of property seizures, although he is quick to add that they were out on bail the following day.[28]

Similarly, Claudio Véliz of the University of Chile, writing in the April, 1971, issue of *Foreign Affairs*, argues that "Chile will not easily abandon the path of democratic legality which President Allende has so emphatically declared to be the one his government is determined to follow," and concludes that Chile, therefore, presents not a threat, but a hope to the United States and the Western Hemisphere. He adds: "Perhaps, if *Unidad Popular* succeeds, it would be well to ponder the advantages of a strong dose of domestic pragmatism to qualify the ideological rigidities which all too often inhibit the political arrangements of nations facing such challenging processes of change."[29]

In a series of revealing interviews appearing in the *New York Times* and elsewhere, Allende himself asserts that, if anything, his regime is *increasing freedom*—both at the level of Chilean foreign policy and, by improving the social, economic, and political status of the common man domestically as well. As to the former, Dr. Allende argues that "the only thing we really want is our absolute independence. We are supporters of self-determination and non-intervention." By this he means that his coalition "wants to increase cultural and commercial relations with the United States," but also to be free to exercise "the right to open relations with Cuba" and other Eastern bloc countries.[30]

[27] Personal interviews conducted during the "Scholar-Diplomat Seminar on Latin America," sponsored by the Department of State in Washington, D.C., January 11–15, 1971.

[28] Rodman, "April in Chile," p. 9.

[29] Claudio Véliz, "The Chilean Experiment," *Foreign Affairs* (April, 1971): 453.

[30] Novitski, "Allende Rejects Totalitarian Rule." Also see C. L. Sulzberger,

President Allende emphasizes that, although Chile wants "the best—the very best relations with the United States" and will never do anything against the United States or contribute to injuring its sovereignty, "we do not accept from anyone, that they come and say, 'No, Sir, you can't have relations with Cuba.' " As for Chile's role in the Organization of American States (OAS), the president continues: "It is a platform which we will use for saying what we think. If we approve of something, we shall say so, and if we disapprove, we shall say so too. *But, we shall neither leave it nor allow it to throw us out*" (italics added).[31]

Domestically, Allende defends his "nationalist, popular, democratic, and revolutionary government that will move toward socialism." "I think," he said, "Socialism frees man. . . . I believe that man is freed . . . when he has an economic position that guarantees him work, food, housing, health, rest, and recreation." Pointing out that one-half of the children in Chile between birth and fifteen years of age are undernourished and that there are 600,000 children who are mentally retarded because they have not had enough protein, Allende states, "We can say that the facts, reality, point to the failure of capitalist governments and Frei's Christian Democratic reformism," and to the need for a redistributive socialist revolution in Chile. Dr. Allende adds, however, that by establishing three distinct economic sectors of state, mixed, and private enterprise, "there is no concentration or centralism here such as that in some socialist countries."[32]

As for freedom of religion, President Allende is emphatic in guaranteeing that "there will be the widest religious pluralism . . . that will be absolutely respected." He continues, "The church . . . is going to be a factor in our favor because we are going to try to make a reality out of Christian thought." Referring to the Revolutionary Left Movement's (MIR) use of violence and their efforts to encourage peasants to take over farm land illegally, Allende asserts: "We have said many times that we have no political agreement or understanding with the MIR.

"Allende, in Interview, Bars Any Base Imperiling U.S.," *New York Times*, March 28, 1971, p. 1.

[31] *Ibid.*

[32] Novitski, "Allende Rejects Totalitarian Rule."

The tactics that they have set . . . for themselves are strictly their own responsibility."[33]

Responding to charges that freedom of the press is being threatened in Chile, Allende telegraphed the Inter-American Press Association (IAPA) that he had always "accepted the right of others to dissent" and assured the association that in Chile there is "absolute respect" for the communications media.[34] Asked in mid-April, 1971 (after his coalition won nearly 50% of the vote in the municipal elections), whether he planned to call a plebiscite to dissolve Congress and give him power to form a unicameral "people's" legislature, Allende insisted that he had no intention of trying it at this time. "I expect that the Congress will meditate on the popular verdict. I expect cooperation. We are not going to become arrogant with the victory we have obtained."[35]

With this backdrop of contrasting arguments, assertions, charges, and countercharges, one of the prime tasks of Nathaniel Davis (new U.S. ambassador to Chile) will be to monitor the direction of Allende's regime and to estimate the future prospects for freedom in Chile. In what must be regarded as more of an "art" than a "science," the U.S. Embassy will probably use as one of its benchmark indicators (or indexes) amendments to the Chilean constitution strengthening the guarantees of civil liberties, which Allende agreed to respect last fall in exchange for Christian-Democrat support in order to take office.

Particularly important to watch will be the rights of citizens to associate freely in the political parties of their choice; the access granted to state-controlled communications media for all the political parties; freedom of the domestic and foreign press (including the establishment of competing state organs), labor unions (particularly the right to strike), and civic associations; the independence (or assaults upon) of the judiciary; and an educational system free of political interference (e.g., discrimination in admissions, revisions of textbooks, favoritism in the advancement of teachers). Also important to monitor will

---

[33] *Ibid.*

[34] "Chilean Dilemma Threatens Survival of Free Press," *IAPA News*, no. 201 (March, 1971), p. 2.

[35] "Chile: Mandate for Allende," *Time*, April 19, 1971, p. 24.

be possible covert attempts to indoctrinate and form political action groups in the lower levels of the military, in factories, offices of the mass media, universities, and in neighborhoods. Possible censorship of domestic and international mail and controls placed upon international travel (by nationals and foreigners) should also be placed high on any index attempting to measure the expansion or contraction of freedom in Chile.

But, as President Allende correctly emphasizes, such an index should *also* seek to measure the progress of mitigating and alleviating circumstances that encourage the "alienation" of the average or marginal man in Chile. For example, the following questions should be asked as objectively and the response measured as accurately as possible: "Is the present regime providing jobs, food, housing, education, health, rest and recreation to more Chileans at a faster pace than ever before?" and "Is the present government functioning to move Chile from a client state status (of either the United States or Russia) to a position of a "floater" (i.e., independent or neutral foreign policy)?" The results of such an exercise in measurement, including all of the factors I have mentioned above, should give us all a better understanding of the future prospects for "freedom," in its broadest sense, in Chile.

APPENDIXES, BIBLIOGRAPHY, INDEX

APPENDIX A

List of Senate Interviews

Political Party	Number of Interviews	Time (minutes)
National Party (6)		
Fernando Alessandri R.	2	150
Francisco Bulnes S.	1	85
Enrique Curti C.	2	75
Pedro Ibáñez O.	1	30
Armando Jaramillo L.	1	45
Juan Luis Maurás N.	1	25
Radical Party (10)		
Humberto Aguirre D.	1	50
Hermes Ahumada P.	1	60
Alberto Baltra	1	60
Luis Bossay L.	2	75
Julio Durán N.	2	160
Humberto Enríquez F.	1	80
Jonas Gómez G.	1	40
Exequiel González M.	2	100
Raúl Juliet G.	1	45
Hugo Miranda R.	1	30
Christian-Democrat Party (12)		
Patricio Aylwin A.	1	75
Ricardo Ferrando K.	1	150

NOTE: NR indicates no reply, WR a written reply.

Political Party	Number of Interviews	Time (minutes)
José Foncea A.	1	75
Renán Fuentealba M.	1	240
Raúl Gormaz M.	1	45
Rafael Gumucio V.	1	60
José Musalem S.	1	90
Alejandro Noemí H.	1	45
Tomás Pablo E.	2	75
Ignacio Palma V.	2	180
Benjamín Prado C.	1	110
Tomás Reyes V.	1	60
Socialist Party (7)		
Salvador Allende G.	2	75
Carlos Altamirano	NR	NR
Raúl Ampuero D.	1	60
María Elena Carrera V.	1	30
Tomás Chadwick V.	1	105
Aniceto Rodríquez A.	2	75
Rafael Tarud S.	2	90
Communist Party (5)		
Julieta Campusano C.	2	60
Carlos Contreras L.	1	60
Víctor Contreras T.	1	70
Luis Corvalán L.	1	60
Volodia Teitelboim V.	1	60
National Democrat and National Vanguard Parties (2)		
Baltazar Castro P. (VNP)	NR	NR
Luis Fernando Luengo E. (PADENA)	1	60
Independents (3)		
Jaime Barros (PC)	1	WR
Sergio Sepúlveda G.	1	85
Julio Von Mühlenbrock L.	1	80
Former Senator (1)		
Roberto Wachholtz A. (PR)	1	150

Political Party	*Number of Interviews*	*Time (minutes)*
Staff (22)		
Iván Auger Labarca and assistant	3	300
Guillermo Canales G.	2	60
Raúl Charlín Vicuña and assistant	2	90
Pedro Correa Opaso	3	240
Rafael Eyzaguirre Echeverría	3	150
Pelagio Figueroa Toro	1	60
Sergio Guilisasti Tagle	2	105
Carlos Hoffman	1	120
José Lagos López	3	120
Alcides Leal	1	60
Jorge Mayo	2	110
Eduardo Mira and assistant (secretary of Constitution, Legislation, Justice, and Rules of the Chamber)	1	30
Jorge Tapia Valdés and assistant	3	200
Rodemil Torres Vásquez and assistant	2	120
Luis Valencia Avaria	1	90
(Two others not named at request)	2	100
Former Staff Member (1)		
Federico Walker	1	90

APPENDIX B

Comments and Questionnaire

Every senator and staff member contained in our sample but one was interviewed personally. The sole exception was a senator who requested a written questionnaire. For the senators interviewed personally, several approaches were employed depending on the author's evaluation of the individual senator (impression as well as background research prior to the actual interview). In some cases, a senator was asked the following series of questions in the same order as they appear here. For others, the order was adjusted if we felt it might improve response. In certain cases (25% of the senator interviews and 75% of the staff), we felt rapport was so good that we gave the respondent the list of questions, to which he responded one by one while we took down virtually verbatim notes. Adapting our approach to the needs of each particular situation seems to us to be a highly practical and productive method to employ when interviewing Latin American elites. As personalities vary, so should the interviewer's technique.

Several of the questions in the following list were adopted directly from Wahlke, Eulau, Buchanan, and Ferguson's study of state legislatures in the U.S. and Richard F. Fenno's list for research on the U.S. House Appropriations Committee. Others were specifically designed for use in Chile. Prior to interviewing senators, the author established several contacts among key staff members, who not only aided in meeting several senators initially, but also provided numerous helpful insights that made our own questions much more significant and effective.

A note should be made on the question of "sensitivity" in interviewing in Latin America. Prior to departure for Chile, we received much advice that suggested that we should not attempt elite interviews in Chile—especially after the Camelot incident. Some scholars are pessimistic about what elites will tell you, and whether it has any validity.

Our experience suggests that elites can and should be interviewed in Latin America—or in Chile, at least. Senators and staff with rare exception gave quite freely of their time even though they faced busy schedules. Several were kind enough to invite my wife and me for dinner and subsequent chats. The Office of Information gave me a desk to work at and provided access to valuable documents, not to mention the "participant-observer" status this provided.

One byproduct of interviewing Chilean senators was the opportunity to experience firsthand the socialization process as it operates in the Senate. One gains a greater sensitivity for the strength of institutional loyalty norms or friendship norms when one effectively participates in the system through interview contact. I know of no more effective way to capture the *ambiente* of an institution.

QUESTIONNAIRE—ENGLISH VERSION

These questions are designed to help me understand how the Senate actually works, so that I may compare it to other legislatures, such as those in the United States, England, Germany, or Italy. The answers you give me will be tabulated in a statistical manner, and no names will be used. What you say will be strictly off the record.

1. Would you say there are unofficial norms, rules, expectations in the Senate, i.e., certain things members must do and things they must not do if they want the respect and cooperation of fellow members?

2. What are some of these rules of the game that a member must observe?

3. If a member does or says the things you mentioned, are there any methods that are used to encourage the member to stop doing so? What are they? Are they effective?

4. How about the president of committees (standing)—what role ought he play in order to be most effective in his job? Is the presidency of a committee a powerful position, or only symbolic? If there is a coalition to form a majority, how do you decide who the president should be? What about floor leaders? (each question then asked)

5. How about the president of the Senate, what role ought he to play in order to be more effective in his job and to have the respect and cooperation of his colleagues?

6. It is said that some standing committees are more important than others in the Senate. Is this so? Which are the three most important and three least important ones in your opinion?

7. Once the number of seats for each political party on standing committees is determined after an election (e.g., 1965), how does your party determine which senators will work on each of the respective committees? Is there competition among your senators to obtain a seat on an important committee? If so, how do you decide who should get the contested seats?

8. When you study a bill in committee, is there a lot of partisanship as on the floor?

9. Once a report on a bill is issued, are all committee members supposed to support the report on the floor—or can one disagree (e.g., if you were against the majority in the committee, may you also object on the floor?)? Is this true for both reports? [There are two on every bill.]

10. If a new senator came to you and asked your advice as to how he ought to behave (standing committee, floor, outside the Sala) in order to be an effective member, what would you tell him? Would you give the same advice for each standing committee? [to determine possible difference in expectations for each committee]

11. Why is replacement of members on standing committees so high? What effect does this have on a committee's ability to study bills?

12. It is often said that there is strong party discipline in Chile. Is this true? Does it vary by party? Does it ever happen that senators, knowledgeable on certain bills being studied in a committee, influence the position their political party takes on that bill? Are there circumstances when you believe it is not necessary for a member to vote with his party? Can you give some examples?

13. As a general rule, does a standing committee have much contact with the executive branch during committee work? Does the executive branch ever meet with the committee before a bill is reported? With members of all political parties on the committee?

14. Would you say that senators who are members of opposing political parties get along well personally? How is that?

15. What do you think the role of the Senate should be in Chile's political system? Are there any changes you would like to see or are you pleased with the way it is?

QUESTIONNAIRE—SPANISH VERSION

Estas preguntas están diseñadas para ayudarme a comprender como el Senado trabaja actualmente, en orden de compararlo con otros parlamentos como los de EE.UU, Inglaterra, Alemania e Italia. Las respuestas que Ud. me de serán ingresadas en listas estadísticas y los nombres no serán mencionados. Lo que Ud. diga estará estrictamente fuera de actas o informes.

1. ¿Hay normas, reglas o expectativas no oficiales dentro del Senado, es decir, cosas que los miembros deben y no deben hacer si quieren el respeto ye cooperación de los otros miembros?

2. ¿Cuales son algunas de estas reglas del juego que un miembro debe observar?

3. ¿Si un miembro hace o dice las cosas que Ud. mencionó, hay algún método el cual se usa para aminar al miembro y no seguir procediendo de esa manera? ¿Cuáles son ellos? ¿Son efectivos?

4. En cuanto a los presidentes de comisiones, ¿qué papel debiera desempeñar un presidente de una comisión para ser más efectivo en su trabajo? ¿Es la presidencia de una comisión un puesto poderoso o solamente simbólico? ¿Y los Comités?

5. En su opinión, ¿que papel debiera el Presidente del Senado desempeñar para ser más efectivo en su trabajo y tener el respeto y cooperación de sus colegas?

6. Se dice que algunas comisiones permanentes son más importantes que otras en el Senado. ¿Es verdad? ¿Cuales son las tres más importantes y las tres menos importantes en su opinión?

7. Una vez que el número de asientos para cada partido político se ha determinado después de una elección (por ejemplo, 1965), ¿cómo determina su partido cuales Senadores trabajarán en cada una de las comisiones respectivas? ¿Hay competencia entre sus Senadores para obtener un asiento en una comisión importante? Si es así, ¿cómo deciden Uds. quien obtendrá el asiento disputado?

8. Cuando Uds. estudian un proyecto de ley en una comisión, ¿hay mucho partidarismo como en la Sala?

9. Cuando un informe sobre un proyecto de ley ha sido cursado, ¿se supone que todos los miembros de la comisión lo apoyarán en la Sala? ¿O puede alguno estar en desacuerdo (es decir, si Ud. estaba contra la mayoría en la comisión, puede Ud. también oponerse en la Sala)?

10. Cuando un Senador recién ingresa al Senado y a una comisión, ¿como aprende las modalidades? ¿Trata alguién de ayudarlo o aprende por sí solo? Si un Senador nuevo viene a preguntarle su consejo en cuanto a como debe comportarse en una comisión permanente para ser un miembro efectivo, ¿que le diría Ud.? ¿Daría el mismo consejo para todas las comisiones?

11. ¿Porqué es tan frecuente el cambio de miembros de una comisión permanente? ¿Qué efecto tiene esto en la habilidad de una comisión para estudiar proyectos de ley?

12. A menudo se dice que hay una fuerte disciplina en los partidos en Chile. ¿Es cierto? ¿Variá según el partido? ¿Ha sucedido que los Senadores en conocimiento de cierto proyecto de ley que se está estudiando en una comisión permanente, ejerzan influjo sobre la posición que un partido político tiene en ese proyecto de ley? ¿Hay circumstancias en que Ud. cree que no es necesario que un miembro vote por su partido? ¿Puede dar algunos ejemplos?

13. Como regla general, ¿tiene una comisión permanente mucho contacto con la Rama Ejecutiva durante su trabajo? ¿Se junta alguna vez la Rama Ejecutiva con la comisión antes que un proyecto de ley sea presentado? ¿Con miembros de todos los partidos políticos?

14. ¿Diriá Ud. que Senadores quienes pertenecen a partidos políticos opuestos se llevan bien o congenian personalmente? ¿Como es eso?

15. ¿Cual cree Ud. que debería ser el papel del Senado en el sistema político chileno? ¿Hay algunos cambios que a Ud. le gustaría ver o está Ud. de acuerdo con la manera como está?

BIBLIOGRAPHY

Books

Agor, Weston H. (ed.). *Latin American Legislative Systems: Their Role and Influence*. New York: Praeger Publishers, forthcoming.

Ahumada Muñoz, Ingrid. *Las comisiones parlamentarias en Chile y otros países*. Santiago: Editorial Jurídica de Chile, 1967.

Almond, Gabriel A., and G. Bingham Powell, Jr. *Comparative Politics: A Developmental Approach*. Boston: Little, Brown and Co., 1966.

Anderson, Charles W. *Politics and Economic Change in Latin America: The Governing of Restless Nations*. Princeton: D. Van Nostrand Co., 1967.

Anderson, Charles W.; Fred R. von der Mehden; and Crawford Young. *Issues of Political Development*. Englewood Cliffs, N.J.: Prentice-Hall, 1967.

Andrade Geywitz, Carlos. *Elementos de derecho constitucional chileno*. Santiago: Editorial Jurídica de Chile, 1963.

Auger Labarca, Iván. *La potestad reglamentaria de las asambleas legislativas*. Santiago: Editorial Universitaria, S.A., 1962.

Barber, James David. *The Lawmakers: Recruitment and Adaptation to Legislative Life*. New Haven: Yale University Press, 1965.

Barnard, Chester I. *The Functions of the Executive*. Cambridge: Harvard University Press, 1956.

Blau, Peter M. *Exchange and Power in Social Life*. New York: John Wiley and Sons, 1964.

Bolados Carter, Alfredo, and Julio Bolados Carter. *Album del congreso nacional de Chile : 1818–1923*. Santiago, 1923.

Bruna Contreras, Guillermo. *Estatuto de la profesión parlamentaria.* Santiago: Memoria de Prueba, Universidad Católica de Chile, 1963.

Campos Harriet, Fernando. *Historia constitucional de Chile.* Santiago: Editorial Jurídica de Chile, 1963.

Coser, Lewis A. *The Functions of Social Conflict.* Glencoe, Ill.: The Free Press, 1956.

Cruz-Coke, Ricardo. *Geografía electoral de Chile.* Santiago: Editorial del Pacífico, S.A., 1952.

Dahrendorf, Ralf. *Class and Class Conflict in Industrial Society.* Stanford: Stanford University Press, 1959.

Dexter, Lewis Anthony. *Elite and Specialized Interviewing.* Evanston, Ill.: Northwestern University Press, 1970.

Diccionario biográfico de Chile (Décima tercera edición). Santiago: Empresa Periodística Chile, 1967.

Easton, David. *A Systems Analysis of Political Life.* New York: John Wiley and Sons, 1965.

Edwards Vives, Alberto. *La fronda aristocrática.* Santiago: Editorial del Pacífico, S.A., 1966.

Engber Álvarez, Víctor. *Los presidentes de las cámaras.* Santiago: Editorial Universitaria, S.A., 1967.

Etzioni, Amitai. *Modern Organizations.* Englewood Cliffs, N.J.: Prentice-Hall, 1964.

Fagen, Richard R., and Wayne A. Cornelius, Jr. *Political Power in Latin America: Seven Confrontations.* Englewood Cliffs, N.J.: Prentice-Hall, 1970.

Fenno, Richard F., Jr. *The Power of the Purse: Appropriations Politics in Congress.* Boston: Little, Brown and Co., 1966.

Finer, Herbert. *Government of Greater European Powers.* New York: Holt, Rinehart and Winston, 1956.

Friedrich, Carl J. *Constitutional Government and Democracy.* Revised edition. Boston: Ginn and Co., 1950.

Fuentes, Jordi, and Lía Cortés. *Diccionario político de Chile (1810–1966).* Santiago: Editorial Orbe, 1967.

Gallardo U., Daniel. *Legislaturas del congreso.* Santiago: Editorial Universitaria, S.A., 1967.

Gil, Federico G. *The Political System of Chile.* Boston: Houghton Mifflin Co., 1966.

Gil, Federico G., and Charles J. Parrish. *The Chilean Presidential Election of September 4, 1964—Part I.* Washington: Institute of Comparative Study of Political Systems, 1965.

Gomez, R. A. *Government and Politics in Latin America.* New York: Random House, 1960.

Gorziglia Balbi, Arnaldo. *Facultades presupuestarias legislativas.* Santiago: Imprenta Lazcano, 1960.

Guillermo Guerra, José. *La constitución de 1925.* Santiago: Establecimientos Gráficos Balcells and Co., 1929.

Halperin, Ernst. *Nationalism and Communism in Chile.* Cambridge: M.I.T. Press, 1965.

Heard, Alexander (ed.). *State Legislatures in American Politics.* Englewood Cliffs, N.J.: Prentice-Hall, 1966.

Heise González. Julio. *150 años de evolución institucional.* Santiago: Editorial Andrés Bello, 1960.

Hirschman, Albert O. *Journeys toward Progress: Studies of Economic Policy-Making in Latin America.* Garden City, N.Y.: Doubleday and Co., Anchor Books, 1965.

Homans, George C. *The Human Group.* New York: Harcourt, Brace and Co., 1950.

Huitt, Ralph K., and Robert L. Peabody (eds.). *Congress: Two Decades of Analysis.* New York: Harper and Row, 1969.

Huntington, Samuel P. *Political Order in Changing Societies.* New Haven: Yale University Press, 1968.

Jacob, Herbert, and Kenneth N. Vines (eds.). *Politics in the American States.* Boston: Little, Brown and Co., 1965.

Jewell, Malcolm E. *The State Legislature: Politics and Practice.* New York: Random House, 1962.

Jewell, Malcolm E., and Samuel C. Patterson. *The Legislative Process in the United States.* New York: Random House, 1966.

Johnson, John J. *Political Change in Latin America: The Emergence of the Middle Sectors.* Stanford: Stanford University Press, 1958.

Kahn, Robert L. *et al. Organizational Stress: Studies in Role Conflict and Ambiguity.* New York: John Wiley and Sons, 1964.

Lagos Escobar, Ricardo. *La concentración del poder económico: Su teoria, realidad chilena.* Santiago: Editorial del Pacífico, S.A., 1965.

Leites, Nathan C. *On the Game of Politics in France.* Stanford: Stanford University Press, 1959.

Lipset, Seymour Martin, and Aldo Solari (eds.). *Elites in Latin America.* New York: Oxford University Press, 1967.

Lira Massi, Eugenio. *La queva del senado y los 45 senadores.* Santiago: Editorial "Te-Ele," 1968.

Manríquez G., Ada I. *El senado en Chile.* Santiago: Editorial Universitaria, S.A., 1965.

Manual del senado. Santiago: Editorial Universitaria, S.A., 1966.

March, James G., and Herbert A. Simon. *Organizations.* New York: John Wiley and Sons, 1958.

Matthews, Donald R. *The Social Background of Political Decision-Makers.* New York: Random House, 1954.

———. *U.S. Senators and Their World.* New York: Vintage Books, 1960.

Matus Benavente, Manuel. *Desniveles entre presupuestos iniciales y presupuestos realizados.* Santiago: Editorial Jurídica de Chile, 1957.

Melnik, Constantine, and Nathan Leites. *The House without Windows: France Selects a President.* Evanston, Ill.: Row-Peterson, 1958.

Méndez Rivera, Jorge. *Los acuerdos del congreso.* Santiago: Editorial Universitaria, S.A., 1962.

Mestelán Gaiñó, Carlos R. *Legislaturas y convocatorias del congreso.* Santiago: Memoria de Prueba, 1937.

Moreno G., Gilberto. *Los comités parlamentarios.* Santiago: Editorial Universitaria, S.A., 1964.

Needler, Martin C. *Latin American Politics in Perspective.* Princeton: D. Van Nostrand Co., 1963.

North, Lisa. *Civil-Military Relations in Argentina, Chile, and Peru.* Berkeley: Institute of International Studies, University of California, 1966.

Oyarzun Gallegos, Sergio. *Comités parlamentarios.* Santiago: Editorial Universitaria, S.A., 1948.

Parrish, Charles J.; Arpad J. Von Lazar; and Jorge Tapia Videla. *The Chilean Congressional Election of March 7, 1965: An Analysis.* Washington: Institute for the Comparative Study of Political Systems, 1967.

Payne, James L. *Patterns of Conflict in Colombia.* New Haven: Yale University Press, 1968.

Peabody, Robert L., and Nelson W. Polsby (eds.). *New Perspectives on the House of Representatives.* Chicago: Rand McNally and Co., 1963.

Petras, James. *Politics and Social Forces in Chilean Development.* Berkeley and Los Angeles: University of California Press, 1969.

Petras, James, and Maurice Zeitlin. *Latin America: Reform or Revolution?* Greenwich, Conn.: Fawcett Publications, 1968.

Pfiffner, John M., and Frank P. Sherwood. *Administrative Organization*. Englewood Cliffs, N.J.: Prentice-Hall, 1960.

Poblete Draper, Luis Ernesto. *El primer congreso nacional*. Santiago: Editorial Universitaria, S.A., 1962.

Porter, Charles O., and Robert J. Alexander. *The Struggle for Democracy in Latin America*. New York: The Macmillan Co., 1961.

El proceso presupuestario fiscal chileno. Santiago: Instituto de Economía, Universidad de Chile, 1958.

Ramos Pazos, Adela. *La función legislativa*. Concepción: Memoria de Prueba, 1965.

Romero Gajardo, Waldo. *Sesiones del congreso*. Santiago: Memoria de Prueba, 1966.

Rose, Richard. *Politics in England*. Boston: Little, Brown and Co., 1964.

Sánchez Risi, Armando. *La legislación delegada*. Santiago: Editorial Universitaria, S.A., 1963.

Schein, Edgar H. *Organizational Psychology*. Englewood Cliffs, N.J.: Prentice-Hall, 1965.

Selznick, Peter. *Leadership in Administration*. Evanston, Ill.: Row-Peterson, 1957.

Silva Bascuñán, Alejandro. *Tratado de derecho constitucional. Vol. 3.* Santiago: Editorial Jurídica de Chile, 1963.

Silvert, Kalman H. *Chile: Yesterday and Today*. New York: Holt, Rinehart and Winston, 1965.

―――. *The Conflict Society: Reaction and Revolution in Latin America*. New Orleans: The Hauser Press, 1961.

Tapia Valdés, Jorge A. *La técnica legislativa*. Santiago: Editorial Jurídica de Chile, 1960.

Thibaut, John W., and Harold H. Kelley. *The Social Psychology of Groups*. New York: John Wiley and Sons, 1959.

Thiesenhusen, William C. *Chile's Experiments in Agrarian Reform*. Madison: The University of Wisconsin Press, 1966.

Urzua Valenzuela, Germán. *Los partidos políticos chilenos: Las fuerzas políticas*. Santiago: Editorial Jurídica de Chile, 1968.

Uslar Vargas, Patricio. *La integración del congreso nacional*. Santiago: Editorial Jurídica de Chile, 1966.

Valencia Avaria, Luis. *Anales de la república. Vols. 1 and 2*. Santiago: Imprenta Universitaria, 1951.

Vera Valenzuela, Mario. *La política económica del cobre en Chile*. Santiago: Ediciones de las Universidad de Chile, 1961.

Verba, Sidney. *Small Groups and Political Behavior.* Princeton: Princeton University Press, 1961.

von der Mehden, Fred R. *Politics of the Developing Nations.* 2d edition. Englewood Cliffs, N.J.: Prentice-Hall, 1969.

Von Lazar, Arpad, and Robert R. Kaufman (eds.). *Reform and Revolution: Readings in Latin American Politics.* Boston: Allyn and Bacon, 1969.

Wahlke, John C.; Heinz Eulau; William Buchanan; and LeRoy Ferguson. *The Legislative System: Explorations in Legislative Behavior.* New York: John Wiley and Sons, 1962.

Wheare, K. C. *Legislatures.* New York: Oxford University Press, 1963.

Williamson Jordan, Luis E. *La evolución del senado en Chile.* Santiago: Imprenta General Díaz, 1937.

ARTICLES AND PERIODICALS

Agor, Weston H. "Senate vs. CORA: An Attempt to Evaluate Chile's Agrarian Reform to Date." *Inter-American Economic Affairs* 22 (Autumn, 1968): 47–53.

Altamirano, Carlos. "El parlamento, 'tigre de papel.' " *Punto Final* 2, no. 55 (May 21, 1968): 1–8 (suplemento).

"Andrés Zaldívar juró como ministro interino de hacienda." *El Mercurio,* March 16, 1968, p. 1.

"Another Blow to President Frei." *New York Times,* April 17, 1967, p. 26.

Cabrera Ferrada, Alejandro. "Voz y silencio de las cifras." *Ercilla,* April 5, 1967.

"Congreso pleno aprobo reformas constitucionales." *El Mercurio,* December 30, 1969, p. 1.

"Consecuencias políticas ante apoyo comunista al reajuste." *El Mercurio,* March 15, 1968, p. 1.

Cope, Orville G. "The 1964 Presidential Election in Chile: The Politics of Change and Access." *Inter-American Economic Affairs* 20, no. 4 (Spring, 1967): 9–21.

Dahl, Robert A. "The Evaluation of Political Systems." In *Contemporary Political Science: Toward Empirical Theory,* edited by Itheil de Sola Pool, pp. 166–181. New York: McGraw-Hill Book Co., 1967.

"Directivas de partidos de oposición rechazan el proyecto de reajuste." *El Mercurio,* March 13, 1968, p. 1.

"El Ejecutivo retiró proyecto de reajuste de la convocatoria." *El Mercurio,* January 31, 1968, pp. 1, 18.

"Escuchar la palabra del FRAP." *Ercilla,* April 5, 1967.

Fenno, Richard F., Jr. "The Internal Distribution of Influence: The House." In *The Congress and America's Future,* edited by David B. Truman, pp. 52–71. Englewood Cliffs, N.J.: Prentice-Hall, 1965.

"Función de la empresa privada destacan dos nuevos ministros." *El Mercurio,* February 24, 1968, p. 1.

Haines, Wilder H. "The Congressional Caucus of Today." *American Political Science Review* 9 (1915): 696–706.

Huitt, Ralph K. "Congress: The Durable Partner." In *Lawmakers in a Changing World,* edited by Elke Frank, pp. 9–29. Englewood Cliffs, N.J.: Prentice-Hall, 1966.

———. "The Congressional Committee: A Case Study." *American Political Science Review* 48 (June, 1954): 340–365.

———. "The Internal Distribution of Influence: The Senate." In *The Congress and America's Future,* edited by David B. Truman, pp. 77–101. Englewood Cliffs, N.J.: Prentice-Hall, 1965.

———. "The Outsider in the Senate: An Alternative Role." *American Political Science Review* 55 (1961): 566–575.

Huntington, Samuel P. "Congressional Response to the Twentieth Century." In *The Congress and America's Future,* edited by David B. Truman, pp. 5–31. Englewood Cliffs, N.J.: Prentice-Hall, 1965.

"Juró el nuevo gabinete." *El Mercurio,* February 16, 1968, p. 1.

Kling, Merle. "The State of Research in Latin America: Political Science." In *Social Science Research on Latin America,* edited by Charles Wagley, pp. 168–213. New York: Columbia University Press, 1964.

Kornberg, Allan. "The Rules of the Game in the Canadian House of Commons." *Journal of Politics* 26, no. 2 (1964): 358–380.

Lindberg, Leon N. "The Role of the European Parliament in an Emerging European Community." In *Lawmakers in a Changing World,* edited by Elke Frank, pp. 101–128. Englewood Cliffs, N.J.: Prentice-Hall, 1966.

Manley, John F. "The House Committee on Ways and Means: Conflict Management in a Congressional Committee." *American Political Science Review* 59 (December, 1965): 927–939.

Matthews, Donald R. "Can the 'Outsider' Role be Legitimate?" *American Political Science Review* 55 (June, 1961): 88–93.

Menges, Constantine C. "Public Policy and Organized Business in Chile:

A Preliminary Analysis." *Journal of International Affairs* 20, no. 2 (1966): 343–365.

"Methods of Electing National Legislatures in South America." Institute for the Comparative Study of Political Systems *Special Memorandum* no. 21. Washington, D.C., n.d.

"Notes and Comments—The Chilean Land Reform: A Laboratory for Alliance for Progress Techniques." *Yale Law Journal* 73, no. 2 (December, 1963).

Nunn, Frederick M. "Chile's Government in Perspective: Political Change or More of the Same?" *Inter-American Economic Affairs* 20, no. 4 (Spring, 1967): 310–333.

Packenham, Robert E. "Legislatures and Political Development." In *Legislatures in Developmental Perspectives*, edited by Allan Kornberg and Lloyd Musolf, pp. 521–582. Durham: Duke University Press, 1970.

Polsky, Nelson W. "The Institutionalization of the U.S. House of Representatives." *American Political Science Review* 62 (March, 1968): 144–168.

"Positivo primer contacto de Sáez con dirigentes políticos." *El Mercurio*, February 23, 1968, p. 1.

"Rechazo de reforma." *El Mercurio*, February 26, 1967, p. 17.

"Reforma para disolver el congreso." *El Mercurio*, January 29, 1967, p. 31.

Ripley, Randall B. "The Party Whip Organizations in the United States House of Representatives." *American Political Science Review* 58 (September, 1964): 561–588.

Rogers Sotomayor, J. "Democracia 'representativa' y representación delegada." *Política, Economía, Cultura* no. 259 (December 15, 1967), pp. 9–10.

Scott, Robert E. "Legislatures and Legislation." In *Government and Politics in Latin America*, edited by Harold E. Davis, pp. 290–332. New York: The Ronald Press Co., 1958.

"Senado versus Frei: Constitución puesta a prueba." *Ercilla*, December 14, 1966, pp. 4–5.

Sigmund, Paul E. "Christian Democracy in Chile." *Journal of International Affairs* 20, no. 2 (1966): 332–342.

Silvert, K. H. "The Prospects of Chilean Democracy: Some Propositions on Chile." In *Latin American Politics: 24 Studies of the Contemporary Scene*, edited by Robert D. Tomasek, pp. 383–398. Garden City, N.Y.: Doubleday and Co., Anchor Books, 1966.

Snow, Peter G. "The Political Party Spectrum in Chile." In *Latin American*

Politics: 24 Studies of the Contemporary Scene, edited by Robert D. Tomasek, pp. 399–412. Garden City, N.Y.: Doubleday and Co., Anchor Books, 1966.

Stokes, William S. "Parliamentary Government in Latin America." *American Political Science Review* 39 (September, 1945) : 522–535.

Sunkel, Osvaldo. "Change and Frustration in Chile." In *Obstacles to Change in Latin America*, edited by Claudio Veliz, pp. 116–144. London: Oxford University Press, 1955.

"Texto completo del discurso del Presidente Frei." *El Mercurio*, December 31, 1969, p. 22.

"Un hecho insólito y mesquino." *Ercilla* (special edition), January 18, 1967.

Wahl, Nicholas. "The Fifth Republic: From Last World to Afterthought." In *Lawmakers in a Changing World*, edited by Elke Frank, pp. 49–64. Englewood Cliffs, N.J.: Prentice-Hall, 1966.

GOVERNMENT PUBLICATIONS

Actas oficiales de las sesiones celebradas por la comisión y subcomisiones encargadas del estudio del proyecto de nueva constitución política de la república. Santiago: Imprenta Universitaria, 1925.

"Acuerdos de los comités." *Boletín de Información Parlamentaria* no. 392. Santiago: OIS, April 27, 1968.

"Cambios ministeriales." *Boletín de Información General* no. 37. Santiago: OIS.

Cuatro mensaje del presidente de la república de Chile don Eduardo Frei Montalva al inaugurar al período de sesiones ordinarias del congreso nacional, 21 de mayo de 1968. Santiago: Departamento de Publicaciones de la Presidente de la República de Chile, May, 1968.

Declaración de los comités comunista, demócrata cristiano, radical y socialista del senado en relación con el estudio del proyecto que legisla sobre las universidades. n.d.

Diario de sesiones del senado, 1900–1968.

"Disposiciones legales y labor que desarrolla la oficina de informaciones del senado." *Boletín de Información General* no. 18. Santiago: OIS, May 31, 1967.

Indicaciones formuladas al proyecto de ley que reajuste las remuneraciones de los empleados y obreros de los sectores público y privado, para el año 1968. Senate bull. no. 23.519.

Informe de la comisión de funcionarios de la secretaría del senado encar-

gada de elaborar un anteproyecto de reforma del reglamento de la cor-
poración. Santiago, 1966.

"Retiro de urgencia." *Boletín de Información Parlamentaria* no. 389. Santiago: OIS, April 27, 1968.

Senado—asuntos pendientes en comisiones al 21 de mayo de 1968. Santiago: Instituto Geográfico Militar, 1968.

Senado—nomina de senadores por agrupaciones provinciales y partidos
políticos—comités parlamentarios—períodos para los que fueron elegi-
dos y sus domicilos—miembros de comisiones. Santiago: Instituto Geográfico Militar, August, 1967.

UNPUBLISHED MATERIALS

Actas de los comités parlamentarios—1965.

Dix, Robert H. "Oppositions and Development in Latin America." Paper
delivered at the 1967 Annual Meeting of the American Political Science
Association, Chicago, September 5–9, 1967. Mimeographed.

Flanigan, William, and Edwin Fogelman. "Patterns of Political Development and Democratization: A Quantitative Analysis." Paper delivered
at the 1967 Annual Meeting of the American Political Science Association, Chicago, September 5–9, 1967. Mimeographed.

Harrill, Ernest Eugene. "The Origins and Institutional Emergence of the
Parliamentary System of Government in Chile." Master's thesis, University of North Carolina, 1949.

Kaufman, Robert Ray. "Chilean Political Institutions and Agrarian Reform: The Politics of Adjustment." Ph.D. dissertation, Harvard University, 1967.

Manley, John F. "The House Committee on Ways and Means: 1947–
1966." Ph.D. dissertation, Syracuse University, 1967.

Membership of Senate Committees and Intra-Legislative Period Replacement: 1965 to September, 1968.

Senate Office of Information Consultations, 1959–1968.

Tape recording of sessions of Secretaría del senado encargada de elaborar
un anteproyecto de reforma del reglamento de la corporación.

INDEX

additive veto: use of, by Frei, 166
Agrarian Reform Bill (1962): 44
Agrarian Reform Bill (1966): support for, 137; mentioned, 41, 44
Agrarian Reform Corporation: 15, 16
Agriculture and Colonization Committee: 70, 85
Aguirre Cerda, Pedro: 110
Aguirre Doolan, Humberto: and Agriculture and Colonization Committee, 85; mentioned, 141
Ahora: 174
Ahumada, Hermes: seniority of, 90; mentioned, 74
Aisén: 165
Alessandri, Fernando: and Constitution, Legislation, Justice, and Rules Committee, 85, 87, 109; and Finance Committee, 88; seniority of, 90; as president of the Senate, 115; on impartiality, 117; specialization of, 151; mentioned, 74, 105, 110
Alessandri Palma, Jorge: as president of Chile, 168; mentioned, 14
Alessandri Palma, Arturo: and composition of Senate, 19; and executive power, 21; and Constitution of 1925, 109; mentioned, 114
Allende Gossens, Salvador: and Public Health Committee, 85; as president of the Senate, 115; on impartiality, 117; as president of Chile, 168–169, 170; goals of, 172; mentioned, 118, 139, 141
Alliance for Progress: 172
Altamirano, Carlos: and Finance Committee, 85; specialization of, 151; on socialization, 153; mentioned, 14, 171

Alvarez, Humberto: and Constitution, Legislation, Justice, and Rules Committee, 87
Ampuero, Raúl: on role of Senate, 143; mentioned, 74, 81, 141, 158
Amunátegui, Gregorio: and Finance Committee, 87; mentioned, 139
Andrade Geywitz, Carlos: on committee function in Senate, 38; on committee rankings, 75
apprenticeship: in Senate, 151–152
Austral University Bill: 45
Aylwin, Patricio: and Constitution, Legislation, Justice, and Rules Committee, 85; specialization of, 151; mentioned, 74, 139

Baltra, Alberto: 85, 99
Bolivia: 177
Bossay, Luis: and Salary Readjustment Bill, 55; and Finance Committee, 85, 88, 96, 109; specialization of, 99, 151; mentioned, 74, 85, 100, 110
Brazil: 18, 177
British House of Commons: political party discipline in, 38
Bulnes, Francisco: conflict of interest charges against, 41; and Constitution, Legislation, Justice, and Rules Committee, 87; and Government Committee, 109; specialization of, 151; mentioned, 39, 53, 110, 119, 120
Burke, Edmund: on French Revolution, 165

Cabero Díaz, Alberto: on impartiality, 117
cabinet: selection of, 3